THE MONASTERY OF SAINT CATHERINE AT MOUNT SINAI

THE CHURCH AND FORTRESS OF JUSTINIAN

PLATES

THE UNIVERSITY OF ALEXANDRIA
THE UNIVERSITY OF MICHIGAN
PRINCETON UNIVERSITY

THE MONASTERY OF SAINT CATHERINE
AT
MOUNT SINAI

George H. Forsyth
Field Director
The University of Michigan

Kurt Weitzmann
Editor
Princeton University

Kelsey Museum

Barr Ferree Foundation

Published with partial subvention from the Barr Ferree Foundation
of the Department of Art and Archaeology, Princeton University, and
from The Kelsey Museum of Ancient and Mediaeval Archaeology, The
University of Michigan

The Monastery of Saint Catherine

THE MONASTERY OF SAINT CATHERINE
AT
MOUNT SINAI

THE CHURCH AND FORTRESS
OF
JUSTINIAN

PLATES

by

GEORGE H. FORSYTH
AND
KURT WEITZMANN

with

IHOR ŠEVČENKO

and

FRED ANDEREGG

THE UNIVERSITY OF MICHIGAN PRESS
Ann Arbor

Πρόλογος

Ἀπὸ τῆς Ἱδρύσεως τῆς Ἱερᾶς Μονῆς τοῦ Σινᾶ κατὰ τὸν ἕκτον αἰῶνα ὑπὸ τοῦ ὁσίας μνήμης Αὐτοκράτορος τοῦ Βυζαντίου Ἰουστινιανοῦ τοῦ Α΄ ἐν τῇ βαθυτάτῃ καὶ ἀγόνῳ καὶ ἀνύδρῳ ἐκείνῃ ἐρήμῳ τῆς Πετραίας Ἀραβίας, συνελέγησαν ἐν αὐτῇ ὑπὸ τῶν αὐτόσε μονασάντων κατὰ καιροὺς Ἑλλήνων Ὀρθοδόξων Μοναχῶν πολυάριθμα μὲν καὶ πολύτιμα χειρόγραφα, πολυπληθεῖς δὲ καὶ πολύτιμοι παλαιοχριστιανικαὶ καὶ Βυζαντιναὶ εἰκόνες, πλὴν ὅμως ὀλίγοι ἐκ τῶν ἐπισκεφθέντων αὐτὴν κατὰ διαφόρους καιροὺς εἰδικῶν ἠσχολήθησαν μὲ τὴν μελέτην τῶν πολυτίμων τούτων θησαυρῶν (Πορφύριος Οὐσπένσκη, Μπενεσέβιτς, Κ. Ἄμαντος, Κοντακώφ, Μ. Χ. Ραμπίνο).

Ἐκτὸς τούτων ὁ καθηγητὴς κ. Γ. Σωτηρίου, προσκληθεὶς ὑφ᾿ἡμῶν τῷ 1938, ἠσχολήθη συστηματικῶς μὲ τὴν μελέτην τῶν σπουδαιοτέρων εἰκόνων καί, βοηθούμενος ὑπὸ τῆς συζύγου του Μαρίας, ἐδημοσίευσεν τῷ 1956 σοβαρὸν δίτομον ἔργον περιλαμβάνον τὰς 238 σπουδαιοτέρας, κατ᾿αὐτόν, εἰκόνας.

Διὰ τοῦτο αἰσθανόμεθα ἰδιαιτέραν καὶ μεγάλην χαρὰν προλογίζοντες τὸ ἑξάτομον μνημειῶδες ἔργον, ὅπερ ἀποτελεῖ πραγματικὸν ἆθλον καὶ προῆλθεν ἐκ τῆς λεπτομεροῦς καὶ ἐπισταμένης μελέτης ὄχι μόνον ὅλων τῶν εἰκόνων τῆς Μονῆς καὶ τῶν Μωσαϊκῶν τῶν εὑρισκομένων ἐν αὐτῇ, ἀλλὰ καὶ τῆς ἀρχιτεκτονικῆς τοῦ κεντρικοῦ Ναοῦ καὶ τῶν ἐντὸς καὶ ἐκτὸς τοῦ τείχους κτισμάτων, τῶν ἐπιγραφῶν, τῶν μικρογραφιῶν, αἵτινες κοσμοῦν πολλὰ χειρόγραφα καὶ κώδικας, καὶ τῶν προϊόντων τῆς ἀραβικῆς τέχνης, ἅτινα ὑπάρχουν ἐν τῇ Μονῇ.

Τὸ ἔργον τοῦτο ἤρξατο τῷ 1958 διὰ κοινῆς προσπαθείας τοῦ Πανεπιστημίου τοῦ Princeton, ἀντιπροσωπευομένου ὑπὸ τοῦ καθηγητοῦ κ. Κούρτ Βάϊτζμανν, τοῦ Πανεπιστημίου τοῦ Michigan, ἀντιπροσωπευομένου ὑπὸ τοῦ καθηγητοῦ κ. Γεωργίου Χ. Φορσάϊτ καὶ τοῦ κ. Φρέντ Ἄντερεγκ, καὶ τοῦ Πανεπιστημίου τῆς Ἀλεξανδρείας, ἀντιπροσωπευομένου ὑπὸ τοῦ καθηγητοῦ κ. Ἄχμετ Φίκρυ.

Ἀπὸ τοῦ 1960 ἀπετέλεσε μέλος τῆς ὁμάδος τῶν ἐν τῇ Μονῇ ἐργαζομένων ἐπιστημόνων ὁ καθηγητὴς τοῦ Πανεπιστημίου τῆς Columbia κ. Ἰχόρ Σεβτσένκο.

Συμμετέσχον ἐπίσης, κατὰ περιόδους, εἰς τὸ ἔργον τῆς Ἐπιτροπῆς, ὁ καθηγητὴς κ. Μανόλης Χατζηδάκης, Διευθυντὴς τῶν ἐν Ἀθήναις Μουσείων Βυζαντινοῦ καὶ Μπενάκη, καὶ ὁ καθηγητὴς κ. Παῦλος Ἄντερβουντ τοῦ Ἰνστιτούτου Dumbarton Oaks τοῦ Πανεπιστημίου Harvard.

Πρόλογος

Καὶ θεωροῦμεν ἐπιβεβλημένον ν᾽ἀπονείμωμεν εἰς αὐτοὺς δίκαιον ἔπαινον καὶ θερμὰ συγχαρητήρια διὰ τὸ θαυμάσιον καὶ πολύτιμον ἐπιστημονικόν των ἔργον, προϊὸν μακρᾶς, πολυμόχθου καὶ εὐσυνειδήτου ἐργασίας, διὰ τοῦ ὁποίου θὰ γίνουν γνωστοὶ εἰς πάντα φιλίστορα οἱ πολύτιμοι ἱεροὶ θησαυροί, οἱ φυλασσόμενοι ἐπὶ 15 ὁλοκλήρους αἰῶνας εἰς τὴν Μονὴν τοῦ θεοβαδίστου ὄρους Σινᾶ.

Ἀλλὰ καὶ εἰς τὰ Πανεπιστήμια τοῦ Michigan καὶ τοῦ Princeton καὶ τὸ μετ᾽αὐτῶν συνεργαζόμενον ἐπὶ τοῦ πεδίου τούτου Πανεπιστήμιον τῆς Ἀλεξανδρείας ὀφείλονται εἰλικρινῆ συγχαρητήρια, διότι διὰ τῆς ὀργανώσεως τῶν εἰς Σινᾶ ἀποστολῶν καὶ τῆς οἰκονομικῆς συμμετοχῆς των εἰς τὴν διαρρύθμισιν τῆς ἐπικουρικῆς Πινακοθήκης τῆς Μονῆς συνετέλεσαν τὰ μέγιστα εἰς τὴν ἐπέκτασιν τῶν γνώσεών μας τῶν σχετικῶν μὲ τὴν τῶν Βυζαντινῶν πρόοδον εἰς τὸν καλλιτεχνικὸν τομέα.

Κάϊρον 10 Ἰουνίου 1965

Ὁ Ἀρχιεπίσκοπος τοῦ Ὄρους Σινᾶ
Πορφύριος Γ΄ (†)

Preface

THIS volume of plates has been published before the accompanying text volume. In both the material is presented in two parts. The first section is the province of Professor George H. Forsyth and will contain everything pertaining to architecture, including sculptural relief in stone and wood. The second will deal with monumental painting, i.e., mosaics, frescoes, and two encaustic paintings on marble, and this part will be the province of Professor Kurt Weitzmann.

In the text volume, now in preparation, the first section will be illustrated with the architectural drawings, more detailed photographs and comparative material, and will seek to reconstruct the form of the Monastery as originally built by Justinian in the sixth century and will relate it to similar buildings of the period. In particular the plan of the church will be studied in relation to the development of pilgrimage churches at Holy Places in Palestine and Syria from the fourth to the sixth centuries. The capitals in the nave of the church will be discussed by Dr. Fawzi el-Fakharani. A chapter will be devoted to analysis of the roof trusses of the church, which prove to be of sixth-century date and therefore unique. The present volume of plates records the surviving parts of the original Monastery and shows it in relation to its natural surroundings, just as the text will discuss it in historical perspective. The second section will deal primarily with the apse mosaic, the history of scholarship which has only gradually come to appreciate it, the iconography of its various parts and its relation to other monuments, the characteristics of its style and its place in the development of Early Byzantine art, an evaluation of its high artistic quality, and, last but not least, the various layers of meaning which make this mosaic one of the most complex creations from the point of view of religious content. Moreover, the text volume will contain contributions by Professor Ihor Ševčenko on the inscriptions to be found on the architecture as well as on the mosaic, a brief sum-

mary of which is included in the present volume, and by the late Professor Paul Underwood and Mr. Ernest Hawkins on the preservation and cleaning of the mosaic. Dr. Abdo Daoud will discuss the frescoes of the Chapel in the Wall.

Among the subsequent volumes now in preparation, several will be devoted to the Monastery's outstanding collection of more than two thousand icons which range from the sixth century to modern times. It is planned to publish the Byzantine icons in the form of a catalogue raisonné completely through the 13th century and to become somewhat selective with the late Byzantine icons of the 14th and first half of the 15th centuries. These sections will be published by Professor Weitzmann. The post-Byzantine icons will be published by Dr. Manolis Chatzidakis and here an even stronger principle of selection will have to be applied in order to separate the icons of first quality from the great mass of average and low-quality icons. Those with Arabic inscriptions and an Egyptian style will be published by Dr. Samy Shenouda. In addition, our expedition has made a complete photographic record of all the miniatures in the library and they will be published in a separate volume by Professor Weitzmann. Another one, by Professor Ševčenko, will deal with the dated manuscripts, and a final volume with the history of the Monastery containing contributions by various scholars.

At the same time our expedition, being basically concerned with archaeological and art historical material, did not wish to include philological material. It therefore abstained from microfilming those texts not included in the photographic record made under the direction of Professor Kenneth W. Clark by the United States Library of Congress Expedition in 1950, which microfilmed the great majority of the manuscripts in the library. This is still an unfinished chapter which we hope will lead to another expedition undertaken by philologists. Finally, we are planning a volume which will contain liturgical and other art objects in the treasure. These will be published selectively since those of the earlier periods, of which the Monastery must once have possessed a wealth, have disappeared except for a few, though important ones; and those of the later periods can claim only limited interest. The Islamic antiquities within the Monastery, notably the mosque with its minaret and the significant Arabic inscriptions will be published under the direction of Professor Ahmed Fikry, retired chairman of the History Department of the University of Alexandria.

It may seem surprising that so famous a monastery as St. Catherine's, favored since its foundation as a goal of pilgrimage because of its location at the traditional site of the Burning Bush of Moses and known for its ancient buildings, its rich library, and its venerable religious monuments, most of which have often been reported by pilgrims, travelers, artists, and scholars, should, with the exception of some famous manuscripts in its library, have been recorded in a comprehensive, scientific way only during the last decades. In 1869 was published the British Ordnance Survey of the Sinai Peninsula, which includes a remarkably accurate record of the topographical setting of the Monastery and of its architectural plan but does not pretend to describe its contents. Just before World War I a German expedition made a photographic survey of it, but the photographs were all destroyed during the hostilities before they could be published. The most comprehensive, scientific monograph on Sinai and its treasures up to the present is that of the Russian scholar Kondakov, who visited the Monastery in 1879.

The reason that the Monastery has had to wait so long for a full-scale investigation is primarily a practical one. Until automobiles and trucks were able to negotiate the treacherous sandy tracks of the Sinai Peninsula, transportation to the Monastery of the heavy equipment required by a large expedition and of the ample supplies needed to sustain it was a formidable task. Before thirty years ago everything had to be transported on the backs of animals. As recently as 1912 Baedeker describes the procedure for assembling a dragoman, camels, tents, food, and water, which were then required for the eighteen-day round trip between Suez and the Monastery, in terms reminiscent of Friar Faber's description of preparations for his trip to Mount Sinai in 1483. Mechanized transportation enabled us to carry thither tons of equipment including electric generators, scaffolding, ladders, surveying instruments, photographic supplies, medicines, and sufficient food to support a dozen people for three months.

There are further reasons why a larger expedition became possible only in recent years. Previous scholars met greater difficulties in gaining access to the precious books of the library, and many of the most important icons had been kept in places apparently unknown. Kondakov mentions only a few, and not the most important ones which undoubtedly he would have recognized as such had he seen them. It is to the credit of Professor George and Mrs. Maria Sotiriou to have published in 1956 in a plate volume, which in 1958 was followed by an accompanying text, a representative selection of the Sinai icons and thus to have introduced a new chapter into the history of Byzantine art. That our expedition was allowed to do more detailed work on this unique icon collection is due, first of all, to the liberal and sympathetic attitude of His Beatitude Porphyrios III, the venerable late archbishop and abbot of the Monastery of St. Catherine. He has shown an active interest in the artistic monuments of the Monastery and he cordially acceded to our request for authorization of the expedition. In addition to giving permission for a complete photographic record, he also authorized our expedition to take the necessary steps for the preservation and cleaning of the great apse mosaic, the uncovering of the Jephthah panel behind St. Catherine's tomb and, in its initial stage, the conservation and cleaning of icons. With great generosity he permitted us to make a complete and detailed architectural survey of every part of the church and fortress and to erect our great metal scaffoldings wherever necessary for this work.

The history of our enterprise can be given briefly. In 1956 The University of Michigan sent a well-equipped Reconnaissance Expedition to make an extensive survey of many archaeological sites in the Near East. At the conclusion of the trip the director of the expedition, Professor Forsyth, then chairman of the History of Art Department, and the photographer, Mr. Fred Anderegg, supervisor of Photographic Services of The University of Michigan, were joined by Professor Weitzmann of the Department of Art and Archaeology of Princeton University and of the Institute for Advanced Study. Together they visited the Monastery of St. Catherine for five days, Professor Weitzmann remaining one month longer for the study of manuscripts and icons. In 1957 Dean Charles E. Odegaard of The University of Michigan, who had sent out the Reconnaissance Expedition, invited Professor Rensselaer W. Lee, then chairman of the Department of Art and Archaeology of Princeton, and Professor Weitzmann to discuss a possible collaboration between the two universities to record and publish the architectural monuments of the Monastery as well as the paintings and other works of art it contains. A joint expedition was then constituted with the aim of organizing a series of campaigns and plans were laid out for a comprehensive publication. For the campaigns of 1958 and 1960 Professor Forsyth was appointed field director, and for those of 1963 and 1965 Professor Weitzmann, who, at the same time, is editor of our publications. All four expeditions were organized technically and were set up at Mount Sinai by The University of Michigan under the supervision of Professor Forsyth, later director of the Kelsey Museum of Archaeology, and of Mr. Anderegg, who was director of all our photography and who not only accomplished the difficult feat of establishing a photographic laboratory in the desert but also took full responsibility for all matters of commissariat, transportation of equipment overseas, and practical logistics. Without his untiring efforts our expeditions would have been impossible. The last two expeditions, in 1963 and 1965, were mainly devoted to photographing icons, illustrated manuscripts, and other works of art under the supervision of Professor Weitzmann. Professor Ševčenko, then of Columbia University, took part in the campaigns of 1960 and 1963 as our Byzantine historian and specialist in epigraphy and palaeography.

The Egyptian government gave its generous assent to our request for authorization of the project. Arriving in Egypt in April, 1958, the joint expedition was fortunate in finding that the University of Alexandria would be interested in becoming a third participant in the enterprise. Since then its name has been the Alexandria-Michigan-Princeton Archaeological Expedition to the Monastery of Saint Catherine at Mount Sinai. The representatives of the three universities were, respectively, Professors Ahmed Fikry, Forsyth, and Weitzmann. After the retirement of Professor Fikry he was replaced by Professor Awwad of the University of Alexandria.

In 1958 our expedition remained at the Monastery for about three months and was very actively engaged in analyzing, surveying, and photographing the architecture and in recording, classifying, and photographing the collections of icons, illustrated manuscripts, and other works of art. During the autumn of 1960 this work was continued at the Monastery for another three months and the photographic record of the architecture was completed. Mr. Robert L. Van Nice was generously given leave of absence from The Dumbarton Oaks Center for Byzantine Studies in Washington so that he could spend a month at the Monastery in 1958 and again in 1960 in order to work with Professor Forsyth on the architectural survey which was completed by the latter during the two final campaigns, in 1963 and 1965, each lasting three months. In 1963 ever-increasing numbers of color ektachromes of the icons, along with the black and white photographs, were most expertly executed by Mr. John Galey of Basel. In 1965 the icon photography was concentrated on those panels that were freed of later overpainting and discoloring varnishes, a project started by Mr. Carroll Wales of Boston and later continued, at the instigation of the Monastery, by Mr. Margaritoff of the Byzantine Museum in

Athens. The mosaic in the sanctuary of the church was inspected by the late Professor Paul Underwood, the director of the Byzantine Institute of America, which immediately undertook the project of preserving and cleaning the mosaic at the expense of an anonymous benefactor. This delicate and exacting work was supervised by Mr. Ernest Hawkins and was carried out with complete success by him and Mr. Carroll Wales, assisted by Mr. Constantine Causis. Subsequently, Mr. Hawkins cleaned the Jephthah panel in the sanctuary of the church and removed its marble frame.

During each of the lengthy campaigns many obligations have been incurred for friendly assistance. First and foremost we wish to acknowledge again our debt of gratitude to His Beatitude Porphyrios III for his gracious authorization of the project and his continuing support of it. Next we wish to thank the Archimandrite Gregorios, the learned secretary of the archbishop, who, after the death of Porphyrios, has succeeded him as archbishop, for his active interest. Furthermore, our thanks go to all the Fathers of the Monastery, in particular to Father Dionysios, the former acting librarian and later oeconomos, for their willingness to spend many hours of their time assisting us during our work in the church, in the library, and in the various rooms which contain icons. They showed an unfailing friendliness in spite of the disruption which our work inevitably caused in their devout way of life. We also wish to express our appreciation of the devoted services of the Beduins attached to the Monastery, who worked loyally in various capacities.

Many debts of gratitude are owed to the authorities and our colleagues and friends in Egypt. In 1958 and 1960 His Excellency Dr. Naguib Hashem, then minister of Education, and Dr. Mohamed Kamel Nahas were very helpful in paving the way for a successful campaign, and in 1963 His Excellency Dr. Abdel Aziz el-Sayed, the minister of Higher Education, continued the benevolent attitude of the Egyptian government. Already in 1960 Dr. Abdel Aziz el-Sayed, while rector of the University of Alexandria, and Mr. Mohamed Kamel Siddik, then executive secretary of the University, had shown a very active interest in our enterprise and had honored us with a visit to the Monastery. An essential factor in our expedition's success was the practical assistance of the vice-rector, Dr. Abdel Fattah Mohamed. In 1965 Professor Mohamed Awwad Hussein continued to show the lively interest of the University of Alexandria in the project.

We wish to acknowledge with sincere gratitude the loyal backing of our two universities. In particular it was Dean Charles E. Odegaard of Michigan who had the imagination and drive to set us on the road that led to Sinai and who thereafter supported us administratively, financially, and with his scholarly interest as a medieval historian. Of equal importance was the enthusiastic backing of Professor Rensselaer W. Lee of Princeton, who likewise perceived with a scholar's intuition the possibilities of the project and who gave his untiring efforts to the promotion of our plans and to the raising of funds from private donors and from charitable foundations.

From the inception of our enterprise we received invaluable advice as to procedure from Professor Aziz Suryal Atiya of the University of Utah, based on his experience as the Egyptian member of the Library of Congress Expedition to the Monastery a few years earlier.

For financial support our expeditions are indebted to many organizations and individuals. First and foremost among the organizations must be mentioned the universities of Michigan and Princeton, the original partners in the enterprise; then the University of Alexandria, the American Research Center in Egypt, the Bollingen Foundation, the Byzantine Institute of America, Columbia University, and the Institute for Advanced Study at Princeton, all of which gave generous and timely financial aid. Of great value was the heartening support of the following individuals: Mr. William Hendrickson, Mr. Arthur Amory Houghton, Jr., and Mr. Frank P. Leslie, all three of whom, not content to make financial contributions, showed their personal interest by visiting our expedition at Mount Sinai.

It is a pleasure to emphasize the important part played by the temporary members of the expedition. Many have been mentioned above. In addition a group of most cap-able and devoted photographers assisted Mr. Anderegg in making the comprehensive photographic record of the architectural features, the works of representational art, the epigraphical and palaeographical monuments, and art objects of many kinds. This group included Mrs. Grace Durfee and Mr. John Galey, who were with us for two seasons, and Messrs. Walter Grunder and Maiteland R. Lamotte, each of whom spent one season with us. Able assistance was also rendered by Mrs. Helen Smith, Miss Elizabeth Grunder, and Mr. Donald McClelland, each of whom was at the Monastery for one season. In 1958 Professor Ralph M. Berry of the Department of Civil Engineering at The University of Michigan assisted Professor Forsyth in the architectural survey.

Finally, it is a pleasant duty to record the most cordial cooperation with those members of the Faculty of Arts of the University of Alexandria who accompanied Professor Fikry to the Monastery for varying lengths of time to take an active part in the work of the expeditions, not only within their own primary field of interest, namely the Islamic art and architecture of the Monastery, but also within the Byzantine field. We should like to express our particular thanks for active cooperation to Dr. Fawzi el-Fakharani, who assisted in many ways, both scholarly and practical, to Dr. Abdo Daoud and Mr. Jusuf Shoukry, and to Dr. Samy Shenouda, who was instrumental in paving the way for the alliance with the University of Alexandria.

GEORGE H. FORSYTH
KURT WEITZMANN

Introduction to the Architecture

by
George H. Forsyth

THE Monastery of St. Catherine is remarkable for its longevity. Built of enduring granite in the sixth century by the Byzantine Emperor Justinian I, the Great, it continues to fulfill his intention of sheltering monks who had congregated at the traditional site of the Burning Bush of Moses near the base of the mountain. To this day monks dwell within its fortified walls, whose original circuit is almost complete, and tend the sacred spot in their midst. Adjoining that spot is their church, Justinian's gift, which appears much as it did in the era of its foundation, with the mosaics of the Transfiguration and of Moses before the Bush and receiving the Law still visible above the altar, with wall paintings of the Sacrifice of Isaac and the Sacrifice of Jephthah's Daughter still surviving to left and right of the sanctuary, and with a whole panoply of Early Byzantine decoration in wood, bronze, and stone still intact elsewhere in the church. Even humble domestic arrangements and service structures of the original monastery are partly preserved. To a remarkable degree it continues to manifest in its form and spirit the intent of the great emperor.

The setting of the monastery is worthy of the epic event it commemorates and the monastic ideal it represents. In the panoramic view on Plate I its stark form stands alone in a narrow valley between granite crags as barren as the moon, the peak on the extreme left being Mount Sinai itself. Drawing closer, as in the Frontispiece, which shows the monastery dwarfed by its mountainous surroundings, one can understand how the uncompromising grandeur of these bare peaks against the sky would have seemed appropriate to supernatural manifestations and would have attracted dedicated men who wished to leave far behind them the transient world of mankind in order to ascend to the eternal world of God.

There is no way of knowing whether this, or some other, is the Mount Sinai referred to in the *Book of Exodus,* nor is there any information as to when hermits began to frequent the valley below it. The first dependable document on the region is the *Peregrinatio* of Etheria, a devout lady who came from her home in a western country, perhaps Spain, to visit Jerusalem and other sacred spots in the Holy Land. The *Peregrinatio* is the account of her trip, which probably occurred in the late fourth century. She describes in detail her ascent of the west side of Mount Sinai, clearly the present one, whereon she passed a night, and her descent on its eastern side, where she probably followed a path similar to the one visible at the left in the panorama (Pl. I). The path led her to the site of the Burning Bush which, she says, "is alive to this day and throws out shoots." The Bush stood in "a very pleasant garden" and behind it, as she approached, was a church. Both Bush and church were under the care of holy men who lived in cells on the surrounding slopes and who provided accommodation for her and for her party. Although the monastery of Justinian would not be built here for another century and a half, its basic pattern as the place where stood the sacred Bush, tended by an eremitical group who maintained an adjoining church and welcomed pilgrims, was established already. The architectural program was essentially complete—save for one feature, defense.

According to various accounts the holy men of the Mountain who welcomed Etheria were soon thereafter subjected to persecutions and massacres by wild tribes. The accounts are unreliable and seem largely fictitious, but they may contain authentic reverberations of that restless movement of peoples along the eastern marches of the later Roman Empire, like besiegers testing the defenses of a fortress. Under Justinian and his predecessors an elaborate defensive system had been erected to counter such threats. Extending all the way from Armenia to the borders of Egypt, its northern sector was designed to withstand onslaughts of the redoubtable Sassanians from Persia and its southern part was intended to blunt the fierce raids of the desert peoples. This system was elaborately contrived as a defense in depth consisting of various fortresses and fortified cities linked by military highways along and across the defensive zone. In arid sectors artful arrangements of cisterns and underground conduits were developed so as to provide the defenders with water and deny it to the attackers. In order to slow down and halt hostile advances every possible impediment was put in their way from the first moment when their approach was announced by signal from advance watchtowers and intelligence posts.

The present fortified monastery at the foot of Mount Sinai appears to have been erected by Justinian as a part of this defensive system. According to a later account he built it merely to protect the monks, at their urgent plea, but a far more dependable, contemporary document states that it was intended for a much larger defensive purpose. The *Buildings*, written by Procopius of Caesarea, says that Justinian erected at the base of Mount Sinai "a very strong fortress and established there a considerable garrison of troops, in order that the barbarian Saracens might not be able from that region, which, as I have said, is uninhabited, to make inroads with complete secrecy into the lands of Palestine proper" (V, viii, 9).

In spite of Procopius' description of the fortress as "very strong," it does not appear as formidable as his phrase suggests. Standing at the base of a slope, its walls could have been dominated by archers from the heights above. While its vulnerable position was, of course, dictated by the site of the Burning Bush near the bottom of the valley, the puzzling fact remains that Byzantine military engineers, famous for their skill in fortification and siegecraft, should have been content to encircle the fortress by a wall unprovided with effective flanking towers. Those on the lower side, facing northeast, are relatively

modern; the original ones on the upper, southwest, side are mock towers, projecting too little to provide enfilading fire along the curtain wall. Probably, such a token fortress was adequate to overawe desert tribesmen. Indeed, Procopius himself says, in explanation of a humble fortification wall elsewhere, "the Saracens are naturally incapable of storming a wall, and the weakest kind of barricade, put together with perhaps nothing but mud, is sufficient to check their assault" (II, ix, 4–5).

Obviously, the architect was greatly inconvenienced by the location of the site of the Burning Bush which, like any holy spot, could not possibly be moved. Since it was located only a short distance up the side of the valley, whose floor is occasionally scoured by flash floods from the heights to the east, he was unable to dispose the square plan of the fortress around the Burning Bush site as its central focus, which would have been a more obvious arrangement, without risking destruction of that part of the fortress which would consequently project on to the floor of the valley and be exposed to torrential runoff. In his effort to avoid such an exposed position the architect has erected the square parallel to the valley floor and as far up the slope as possible, accepting a lopsided composition wherein the site of the Bush is at one side of the square and in its lowest part (Figures A, B; Pl. III). Due to the slope Justinian's architect built terraces, carried on great arches, at the bottom of the slope so as to equalize the level of the area within the monastery (Pls. XIX–XXI).

The original outer wall of the monastery can be traced through its whole perimeter, under later remodelings and superstructures, and on three sides it rises to its original height (Pls. IV A, V B, XII A, and Figure A). In many places its battlements are still in position. Its surface is enlivened by decorative carved panels, also of sixth cen-

KEY TO PLAN IN FIGURE A

1. Porch (originally, postern)
2. Original portal (blocked)
3. Entry (under guest wing)
4. Court
5. Covered passage (medieval vault)
6. Court and steps down to church
7. Mosque (converted sixth-century hall)
8. Minaret
9. Storeroom (sixth-century antechamber)
10. Complex of sixth-century arches in basement at southwest corner
11. Rainwater drain (sixth century) running northwest under road and to garden
12. Modern kitchen and service quarters in northeast corner (above sixth-century kitchen)
13. Well of Moses
14. Uncovered passage at lower level
15. Uncovered passage at upper level
16. Church

17. Court
18. Kléber's Tower (early nineteenth century)
19. Modern living quarters and reception room of head monks, in northwest corner
20. Terrace (on sixth-century arches)
21. Guest wing (nineteenth century)
22. Former latrine tower in southeast wall
23. Present refectory (medieval)
24. Modern living quarters of monks (against southeast wall) communicating by verandahs
25. Court above modern bakery
26. Tunnel under 29
27. Tunnel under 29
28. Chapel (sixth century) in southwest wall
29. Structures of various uses and dates (post sixth century)
30. Court (well at center)
31. Modern building on sixth-century wall
32. Ramp mounting from 4

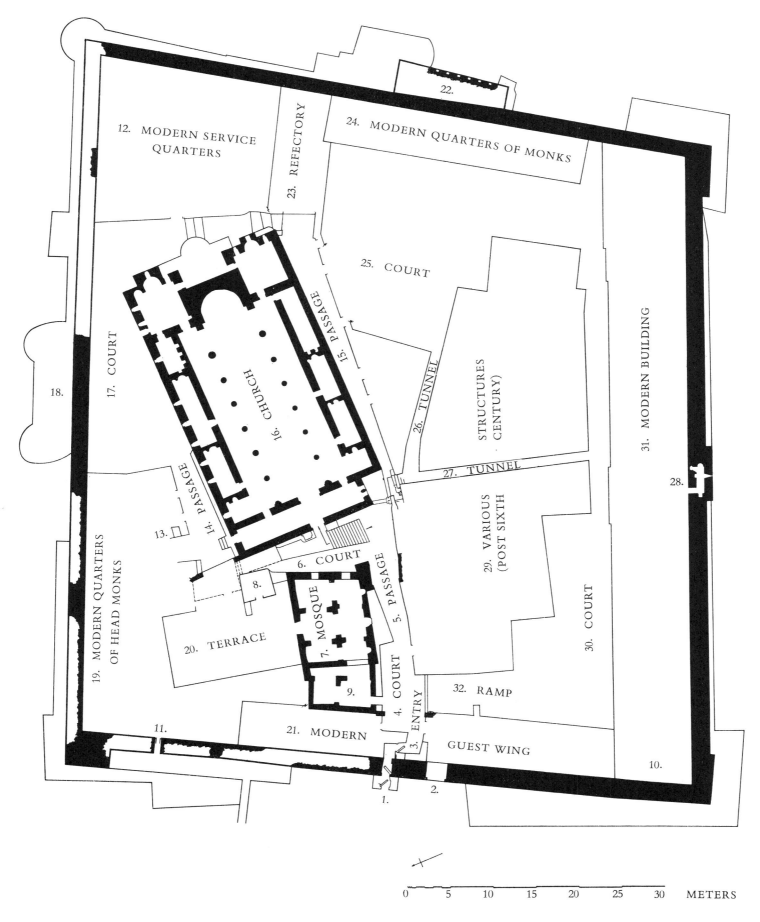

12. MODERN SERVICE QUARTERS

23. REFECTORY

24. MODERN QUARTERS OF MONKS

22.

25. COURT

15. PASSAGE

17. COURT

18.

26. TUNNEL

16. CHURCH

STRUCTURES CENTURY)

31. MODERN BUILDING

14. PASSAGE

13.

27. TUNNEL

28.

6. COURT

8.

29. VARIOUS (POST SIXTH

19. MODERN QUARTERS OF HEAD MONKS

20. TERRACE

7. MOSQUE

5. PASSAGE

9.

30. COURT

32. RAMP

4. COURT

ENTRY

11.

21. MODERN

3.

GUEST WING

10.

1.

2.

0   5   10   15   20   25   30   METERS

A. Mt. Sinai, Monastery of St. Catherine. Plan showing Sixth-century Elements in black and in heavy outline (Key on page 6)

7

tury date, which are set above slit windows (Pls. VIII A, X, XI A, C–D, E). The main entrance, located at the center of the wall's northwest side, was a double one consisting of a large and imposing portal, now walled up, and a postern to the left of it, now preceded by an eighteenth-century porch; the portal was crowned by a flat arch with decorative roundels at each end and must have been closed by a massive door (Pl. XII A–B). Inside the portal and postern is a porch opening into a narrow court, and beyond it is an arched passage which invites the visitor to advance to the corner of the church visible through the passage (Pl. XIV). On the left of the narrow court is the original guest house, first designed as a two-story structure of oblong plan, with an antechamber, but converted to a mosque and provided with a square minaret in the eleventh century as a concession by the monks to the Islamic world around them (Pls. XV B, XVI–XVIII).

In that part of the monastery which is to the right of its main portal, on entering, an open space may have been reserved as a courtyard. No trace of early structures is found in that area. As a pilgrimage center the monastery was in part a caravansary and may well have included within its sheltering walls an open area for all the multitudinous activities of arriving and departing groups of pilgrims.

Continuing on the route from the portal of the monastery to the façade of the church, a visitor advances through the arched passageway and is surprised to find the church sunk deeply in the ground (Pl. XXV). As indicated by outcrops of live rock round about, this submergence is not due to a rise in ground level. Rather, it is caused by the fact that the site of the Burning Bush is in the lowest part of the whole monastery and therefore the floor of the adjoining church was established at about that level, a good four meters below the ground level of the portal of the monastery and of the approach from it to the church. A flight of steps leads from the upper level down to the church door; the steps are relatively modern, but probably reproduce the original flight (Pls. XV B, XXIV).

In order to offset as much as possible the effect of submergence, the façade of the church was heightened by increasing the vertical proportions of its interior beyond the norm and by making the gables inordinately high, much higher than the roof ridge, and by erecting at the corners two towers which seem to be purely for vertical effect (Pl. XXV). The campanile on the left-hand tower was a gift from Russia nearly a century ago.

After descending the steps from the upper level and entering the door of the church, the visitor finds himself in the narthex. Facing him across the narthex is the great inner portal of the nave (Pl. XLIII). The view of the nave is now obstructed by chandeliers and a huge iconastasis of the seventeenth century, but originally the mosaics over the altar would have been visible for the full length of the nave, confronting a visitor from the moment he entered the great western portal (Pl. CIII). Overhead the roof rests on thirteen wooden trusses which were originally visible from the floor of the church, as indicated by carved Crosses and decorative moldings applied to the upper members of the trusses (Pls. LXXXII–LXXXIII). Three of the horizontal beams are inscribed, on their vertical faces, with invocations on behalf of the Emperor Justinian, his Empress Theodora, and the architect of the church, Stephanos (Pls. LXXX–LXXXI). Since the first inscription implies that Justinian was still alive, while the second indicates that Theodora was already dead, the church must have been commissioned between the years in which each died, that is, between 548 and 565. It is a rare piece of good fortune that so well preserved a church should also be a signed and dated work. The trusses and inscriptions, although perfectly intact, are no longer visible from the floor of the church because of later ceiling panels. Luckily, the panels were hung between the horizontal beams, not under them, and therefore do not conceal the bottom surfaces of the beams on which may still be seen the sixth-century carvings of floral ornament and of animals, sea creatures, and river scenes. Bulls, water fowl, crocodiles, boars, rabbits, foxes, deer, hunting dogs, an elephant, a camel, and a gazelle are rendered realistically and with gusto and playfulness. Lively human figures, probably *erotes*, in boats are sailing and paddling frantically. There are even tritons who carry Crosses over their shoulders (Pls. LXVI–LXVII *et seq.*). Although the carvings were garishly painted with heavy coats of red and gold at a later date, traces of earlier staining with red, green, blue, and black can be detected in areas not covered by the later

KEY TO PLAN IN FIGURE B

A. Narthex
B. Nave
C. North aisle
D. South aisle
E. Sanctuary
F. Apse
G. Sacristy
H. Storeroom
　　Chapels in Church
I. Burning Bush (medieval)
J. St. James the Less
K. Forty Martyrs (Holy Fathers)
L. St. Antipas
M. SS. Constantine and Helen
N. St. Marina
O. SS. Anne and Joachim
P. St. Simeon Stylites
Q. SS. Cosmas and Damian

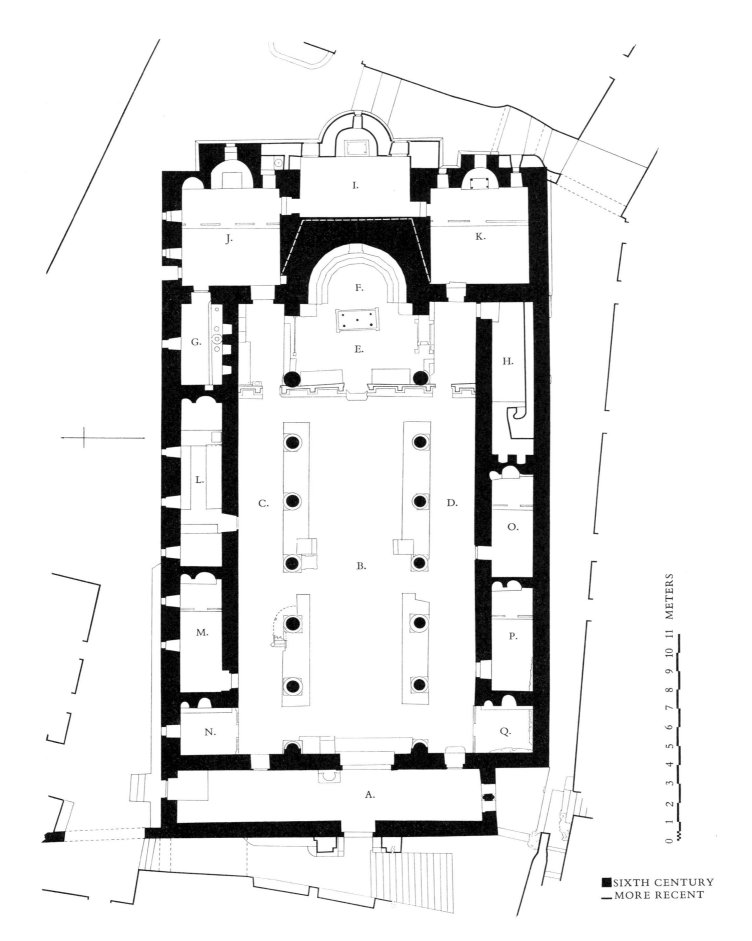

B. Church. Plan showing Sixth-century Elements in black (Key on page 8)

paint. These may be original colors applied when the carvings were new.

The use of animal motifs in decorative sculpture was not limited to the ceiling beams. At both sides of the main altar are marble panels on each of which is represented in low relief a Cross between two deer confronted in a heraldic type of composition (Pl. LXXXVI). Although subsequently reset, the panels appear to have formed part of a chancel rail which originally surrounded the altar table (Pl. LXXXVII A).

Animal carvings also appear at the other end of the church among the decorative details on the great wooden door which opens from the narthex into the nave (Pl. XLVI et seq.). Its four valves contain panels each of which bears on its outer face, toward the narthex, a carving of a bird or animal. Monkeys, gazelles, eagles, rabbits, and a cock are depicted in the same style and with the same charm and animation as their counterparts on the ceiling beams. No doubt they all formed part of the original décor of the church.

To right and left of the sanctuary are handsome original doors sheathed in bronze which give access from each side aisle to large square chapels placed at the corners of the church in such a way as to flank the main apse and also to project well to the east of it (Pls. XCIV–XCIX, cf. Pls. XXXV–XXXVI). These corner chapels, which formed part of the sixth-century plan of the church, now give access to the Chapel of the Burning Bush, situated between them and behind the main apse (Pl. C). Originally, however, there was no Burning Bush Chapel but, in its stead, a small unroofed area at the foot of the main apse, like a diminutive court or open bay, accessible through doors from the corner chapels; and in the court would have stood the Bush itself, ever flourishing, as in Etheria's day. Evidently, pilgrims passed from the aisles into the corner chapels and thence through the doors which led out to the court of the Burning Bush behind the main apse. A medieval traveler reports that the Bush finally disappeared, having been torn apart for relics, and was replaced by a memorial in a chapel, which is the present-day Chapel of the Burning Bush, occupying the place of the original court, and within it is an altar over a slab marking the spot where the Bush once grew (Pl. CI).

Not only has it been possible to discern the main outlines of the original monastery, but many details survive which enable us to have some idea of daily life within it in the sixth century. We conjectured above that a pilgrim entering the main gate of the monastery would see a guest house on his left and an open space on his right which may have been a service court. A system of arcades in the right-hand corner of that space and adjoining the outer wall suggests by its arrangement a storehouse of some kind (Pl. XIX c-d). On the far left, behind the guest house, is found an upper arcade which rises above the original terrace, implying an important superstructure. Perhaps the abbot and chief monks resided in this area, which is occupied at the present day by the governing body of the monastery. In the area beyond the church and therefore as far as possible from the mundane world of caravans and pilgrims, are considerable evidences of domestic activity, which may indicate that the principal living quarters of the monks were in this section, just as they are at the present day. Here we have found in the basement a great kitchen with the original sixth-century oven, food storage vault, and well (Pls. XXI–XXIII). A medieval refectory which stands at one end of the kitchen, at a higher level, may be a replacement of the earliest one (Pl. XXXVIII A). Against the outer face of the adjoining wall of the monastery stands a big latrine tower, no longer in use and largely reconstructed but apparently forming part of the original monastery; six drains are still visible and probably there were eight originally (Figure A no. 22).

A difficult problem is presented at the monastery by the uncertainties of the rainfall. Rarely is there any rain, but it can occasionally descend in torrents producing the dreaded flash floods, sometimes thirty feet deep, which scour the mountain gorges and leave ruin behind them. During the total period of time our four expeditions were at Mount Sinai, about a year in all, we witnessed only two hard downpours, each lasting but a short time. The monastery has always depended for its water supply on cisterns which collect such rainwater as does fall but which must, in view of the scarcity of rain, be fed also by underground seepage from the heart of the mountain.

During a rainstorm the ingenious drainage system of the monastery becomes apparent. Terraces and passages which have seemed level prove to be gently sloping so as to feed the collected waters into convergent streams which, like an arterial system, finally pour into a single drain leading to a subterranean arch in the foundations of the fortress (Pl. XX B). Thence the water flows through an underground channel to a reservoir in the gardens. Without doubt this drainage system formed part of the original design of the monastery. The subterranean arch is clearly contemporary with the wall it penetrates, and the church has a complete system of stone rainspouts, also original, which collected water from the roof and threw it clear of the walls below.

Although later constructions and reconstructions have much altered original arrangements, it is still possible to obtain a better idea here at Mount Sinai than anywhere else of a complete Early Byzantine fortified monastery, as it looked and as it functioned.

Introduction
to the Mosaics and Monumental Paintings

by
Kurt Weitzmann

Aɴ imperial edict of the year 726 forbade the making of holy images within the borders of the Byzantine Empire and ordered all existing ones to be destroyed. This order affected not only icons, in the proper sense of the word, but also figurative mosaics and fresco paintings of religious content. As the result of this edict the destruction of the condemned paintings was, at least in Constantinople, so complete that not a single one seems to have escaped the furor of the iconoclasts.

In a side room on the south gallery in the church of Hagia Sophia in Istanbul mosaic medallions from the preiconoclastic period can still be seen from which the representations of human busts were scratched. Only outside the capital and especially beyond the frontiers of the Empire, where the imperial decrees could not be enforced, did mosaics survive, and this applies in particular to those countries which at the time of iconoclasm already were under Moslem domination. The mosaics were not even covered with plaster as was done later by the Turks in the churches of Constantinople and elsewhere in the Byzantine Empire.

One splendid example of preiconoclastic mosaic decoration, whose survival in perfect condition we owe to the religious tolerance of the Moslem overlords and perhaps also to their antagonism towards the Byzantine emperor, is preserved in the apse of the basilica of the Monastery of St. Catherine on Mount Sinai and in the triumphal arch and wall above it. It is not the only mosaic that has survived in Moslem territory, there being others on Cyprus, the island which was, temporarily at least, controlled by the Moslems. The apse decoration of two Cypriote churches, the Panaghia Kanakaria in Lythrangomi with the Virgin enthroned and the Panaghia Angeloktistos at Kiti near Larnaka with a standing Virgin, both flanked by angels, bear witness to the high standards of mosaic art in the Byzantine Empire before the outbreak of iconoclasm. To be sure, the style of these two mosaics bears only a faint resemblance to that of the Sinai mosaic, the first most likely being earlier, the second later, though no precise dates have, so far, been proposed. Although we cannot determine the date of the Sinai mosaic on stylistic grounds alone, the history of the monastery nevertheless provides some clues based on archaeological evidence.

The basilica was erected and roofed within the lifetime of Justinian as indicated by the carved inscriptions on the beams, one commemorating the death of Theodora († 548), the other referring to the living emperor and imploring his salvation († 565) (Pls. LXXX–LXXXI). The building of a monastery 5000 feet above sea level in the granite wilderness of the Sinai peninsula must have posed great problems of transportation. To move all the materials except the locally cut granite blocks of which the church, the walls, and some edifices within the monastery were built, required a major effort which could not readily be repeated. Apparently, the entire decoration for the church, the marble revetment and chancel panels, the mosaic decoration, and the carving of door panels and beams, was accomplished within a short period and presumably still in Justinian's lifetime, when large funds were made available by this enterprising and energetic builder, who also had Hagia Sophia erected in the astonishingly short time of five years. It is significant that in the post-Justinianic period, presumably in the seventh century, the expansion of the apse program was undertaken not in mosaic but encaustic painting on the marble revetment (Pls. CLXXXVIII–CXCIII). Also, only one other mosaic was ever made and that was done centuries later and is of very low quality, namely the mosaic in the apse of the Chapel of the Burning Bush (Pl. C). Furthermore, it is reasonable to assume that the conquest of Egypt including the Sinai peninsula by Islam only a few years after the Hegira would have impeded any major artistic effort for some time thereafter. Moreover, there are indications that even the immediate successors of Justinian somewhat neglected the patronage of this imperial foundation. All these considerations seem indeed to point to a rather short period of very concentrated effort in which the church was embellished. None of the later additions, of which there are many, ever reached the splendor and high level of those of the Justinianic age. The very high quality of the mosaic decoration presupposes the presence of artisans trained in a long tradition of a metropolitan center, and since the monastery was an imperial foundation, one may reasonably assume that the mosaic artists came from the capital.

It is in line with early church construction and with that of the High Middle Ages in general that the apse or the whole bema should have preferential treatment with regard to marble revetment and mosaic decoration. One need only refer to San Vitale and San Apollinare in Classe in Ravenna, created in the period approximately contemporary with Sinai, or to the two churches in Cyprus already mentioned. As evidence of a continuation of this custom it may suffice to cite the church of Hagia Sophia in Kiev or the cathedral of Cefalù. In some of these cases the nave never received any decoration, while in others fresco painting was chosen. As far as Sinai is concerned, there is no evidence that the nave or aisles had any figurative decoration. The description of a mosaic over the entrance door in travel books of the fifteenth and sixteenth centuries led us to test the west wall in 1963 for remnants of a lost mosaic, but not the slightest trace was found.

When one enters the church today, the view into the apse is hidden by the seventeenth-century carved wooden iconostasis (Pl. XLIII), which is surmounted by an enormous Crucifixion group that reaches to the ceiling and is held in place by a big beam which cuts right across the view into the bema. At the time of Justinian the original iconostasis was most likely executed in marble and quite low, so that the attention of the visitor entering the central door of the church would have been immediately directed toward the fully visible mosaic in the conch of the apse and the wall above it. To a large extent this experience could be made possible again if the decision of the authorities of the monastery to remove the enormous Crucifixion group should be realized.

Standing in the bema behind the iconostasis the beholder's mind will instantaneously be absorbed by the monumental representation of the Metamorphosis which fills the conch of the apse (Pls. CIII, CXXXVI–CXXXVII). Christ stands on the axis within an aureola whose intense blue color isolates him effectively from the gold ground and heightens the luminiscent effect of his garment ("...and his raiment was white and glistering" Luke IX, 29). So dominant is the golden surface area that it leaves only a rather narrow groundstrip as a reminder that the

Transfiguration on Mount Tabor took place on earth. The silver rays emanating from the aureola pass over the two prophets flanking Christ and the three disciples who had accompanied him and change the colors of the garments where they cross them. All five figures share the same groundline and are placed around the aureola in a rhythmic order which greatly contributes to the monumental and balanced impression of the composition. Moses at the right and Elijah at the left each raise one hand in a gesture of speech ("And, behold, there talked with him two men, which were Moses and Elias" Luke IX, 30). Their firm stance contrasts effectively with the kneeling positions of John and James, which correspond with each other, and Peter who has been lying asleep on the ground and, under the impact of the vision, is just awakening ("But Peter and they that were with him were heavy with sleep" Luke IX, 32).

That this mosaic was laid out and in part also executed with the highest artistic skill by the leading artist of an eminent atelier is apparent in many ways. First of all, he perceives the event as one of an inner vision rather than of a physical phenomenon as it is always represented in later Byzantine art, in which the light of Tabor blinds the apostles so much that they try to protect their eyes against the glare. In the subtle Sinai mosaic John and James express astonishment by their outstretched arms (Pls. CX–CXI, CXLVI–XLVII) while Peter on the ground, without abandoning the position of resting his head in the palms of his hands, merely turns his gaze toward the vision with no sign of fear or emotion (Pls. CXIV, CL).

Another indication of the artist's great sensitivity is his pictorial differentiation between Christ, the prophets, and the apostles in their physical reality. Christ (Pls. CIV, CXXXVIII–CXXXIX) has the most dematerialized body which, though showing such details as the free leg and the veiled left hand, is comparatively two-dimensional and centered on an axis. Moses and Elijah have heavier and more solid bodies and their vivid gestures of speech and facial expressions suggest perception of the surrounding world. They are rendered in what one might call a second degree of physical reality. A third degree is used for the three disciples. The contrappostic element in the kneeling poses of John and James (Pls. CX–CXI, CXLVI–CXLVII) leads to a marked emphasis on the upper legs as three-dimensional masses jutting out of the picture plane, and in the posture of Peter (Pls. CXIV, CL), with his right knee drawn up and his left leg extended, suggests stretching at the first moment of awakening and thus introduces a remarkably naturalistic element, justified by the textual source.

Our artist is equally subtle in his characterization of the faces. Christ's face is the most abstract (Pls. CV, CXLI).

The geometric design of the eyes, the arched brows, nose, and beard render this face immobile, without emotion and thus devoid of any human quality. The artist uses abstraction in order to express the nonhuman, i.e., the divine nature of Christ. This conscious effort immediately becomes clearer by contrasting the Christ head with the heads of Moses and Elijah (Pls. CVIII–CIX, CXLIV–CXLV), who look at Christ out of the corner of their eyes with human awareness. They are differentiated: Moses looks with inner calm, Elijah with an expression of great pathos. The same distinction is made between John and James but in reverse (Pls. CXII–CXIII, CXLVIII–CXLIX): John, at the left, wears an expression of utter calm and James, at the right, has one of anxiety. By such a chiastic device the artist achieves a balance of emotional expressions that matches the compositional harmony.

It is a traditional feature of apse and bema compositions to depict the twelve apostles in framing medallion busts (Pls. CIII, CXXXVI–CXXXVII): in the Kanakaria on Cyprus they frame the apse with the Virgin enthroned, in San Vitale in Ravenna they occupy the arch leading into the sanctuary. In Sinai the framing apostle series is very closely integrated thematically with the Metamorphosis in that the three disciples of the Tabor scene, i.e., Peter, John, and James, are not repeated in the medallions, but replaced by the two evangelists Luke and Mark and by Matthias. Moreover, the witnesses of the New Dispensation are supplemented at the bottom by those of the Old, i.e., by the major and minor prophets to whom the bust of David is added in the center (Pls. CXIX B, CLXX).

In the representation of the apostles as well as the prophets the artist displays his ability to depict faces full of character: some are square, bald, and energetic like Jonah (Pls. CXIX A, CLXVI B), others, like Jeremiah (Pl. CLXII B), have thick black hair and the piercing eyes of a religious fanatic. Others, like Andrew (Pl. CXVI A, CLIV A), show an expression of pathos, not unlike that we noticed in the faces of Elijah and James of the Metamorphosis (Pls. CVIII, CXIII, CXLIV, CXLIX). Indicative of the clear, tectonic organization of the frame is the addition of four further medallions which mark the axis and the corners. Placed above the head of Christ is a simple golden cross (Pl. CLII) and below him the bust of his royal ancestor David in the guise of a Byzantine emperor with a purple chlamys and a jewel-studded crown (Pls. CXIX B, CLXX). In the corners we see at the right Longinus (Pls. CXXI, CLXI), whom the dedicatory inscription at the bottom of the Metamorphosis (Pls. CLXXII–CLXXIII) names as the abbot in whose reign the mosaic was executed, and at the left the Deacon John (Pl. CXX–CLX). Unfortunately, their dates are unknown. These two medallions, which represent the donors of the mosaic with

square nimbi, indicating that at the time of its execution they were still among the living, show another aspect of the artist's range of expression. Here he is not portraying character faces as in the case of the apostles and prophets, but individual features with a sense of sharp psychological observation: the sensitive, intellectual face of the Deacon John, whom some scholars have proposed identifying with the famous John Climacus, author of the Scala Paradisi, is effectively contrasted with the energetic face of Longinus with high cheekbones, apparently a man of action.

Moving up from the apse into the triumphal arch (Pls. CIII, CXXXVI–CXXXVII, CLXXIV) one sees on the same axis as Christ and the cross medallion of the conch yet another, but smaller cross medallion against which is set the Lamb of God in three-quarter view (Pls. CXXII A, CLXXV). Its head is turned so as to fit perfectly into the shape of the disc. Two angels with peacock wings, filling the spandrels, are flying toward the center to offer the scepter and orb to Christ (Pls. CXXII B, CXXIII B, CLXXVI, CLXXVII) in quite the same manner as flying Victories in the spandrels of an imperial triumphal arch offer the very same attributes. Small crosses as terminals of the scepters and on the globes are the only changes made to fit a symbolic representation of imperial iconography into that part of the church for which, significantly, the term "triumphal arch" has been adapted from the imperial symbolism. The lower parts of the spandrels are filled with two medallion busts (Pls. CXXIV–CXXV, CLXXX–CLXXXI) whom the monastic tradition has identified to the present day with Justinian and Theodora, an identification obviously reflecting the desire to have the founders of the monastery depicted somewhere in the church as, indeed, they were integrated into the decorative program of San Vitale in Ravenna. There can be no doubt, however, that these medallions depict the Virgin and John the Baptist, effectively set against a silver background.

In these two medallions we see the artist using a similar device as in the Metamorphosis for distinguishing between the divine nature of Christ and the human nature of the prophets and disciples. Like Christ's, the Virgin's face is motionless and designed abstractly, while that of John the Baptist shows great pathos, more intense even than that of Elijah and James in the Metamorphosis (Pls. CVIII, CXIII, CXLIV, CXLIX). The sharp contraction of the brows, the very deep-set eyes, the full and disheveled hair flowing over the shoulders give the impression of a tragic mask and we believe that, indeed, the artist tried to incorporate the reminiscence of an ancient mask in order to convey the impression of John as the tragic prophet.

The uppermost zone of the eastern wall contains two scenes from the life of Moses to the left and right of a

13

double window, which is encased in a rich ornamental border and divided by a column, whose bases, capital, and ornamented shaft are executed in mosaic that pictorially imitates these architectural members (Pls. CXXIX, CLXXIV, CLXXXVII). At the left Moses is seen loosening his sandals before the Burning Bush and looking up to the commanding hand of God issuing from a segment of heaven (Pls. CXXVI, CLXXXII, CLXXXIV). The high rock behind Moses' back suggests that the artist was, indeed, influenced by the actual landscape, i.e., the granite mountains of Sinai. This is even more true of the right scene in which Moses, receiving the tablets of the law in the form of a parchment scroll, is shown standing within a deep mountain gorge (Pls. CXXVII, CLXXXIII, CLXXXV).

To be sure, this rather large surface area covered with mosaics required the teamwork of a whole group of mosaicists and a closer look reveals that the quality differs. To make a sharp distinction among the segments, however, is almost impossible because the principles of medieval workshop tradition were not such that individual artists were commissioned to execute certain parts of the surface area independently. The varying levels of skill were apparently used more economically in such a way that the main artist concentrated on the heads, which are usually executed with smaller cubes, while some assistants made the garments and the least trained just the background. In spite of such a generalization, it can be observed that the best hands concentrated on the Metamorphosis. The medallion of John the Baptist (Pls. CXXIV, CLXXX) stands out also as a work of exceptional quality, while the two flying angels in the same triumphal arch (Pls. CXXII B–CXXIII, CLXXVI–CLXXIX) are the work of comparatively weaker hands. Similarly, the two Moses figures in the top zone (Pls. CXXVI–CXXVIII, CLXXXII–CLXXXVI) are not quite as refined as the figures of the Metamorphosis. Yet there is a uniformity in the technique which leaves no doubt that the whole mosaic surface was executed within an apparently rather short period.

The wealth of artistic forms and expressions has its counterpart in the complexity of the content. This, however, may only to a limited degree be due to the merit of the artist, and to a larger extent that of a learned cleric who, as was customary in Early Christian and Medieval times, advised the artist on the accuracy of the iconography and supplied him with the basic and, in this case, manifold ideas. There are, if one may use a simile, several "layers" of meaning which only an intensive study can unravel, and even then one cannot be sure whether all possibilities of exegesis have been exploited.

The first iconographical aspect which a good many

apse mosaics of the Early Christian period, both East and West, have in common is the eschatological outlook. A portrayal of Christ in the apse, the spherical shape of which suggests heaven, is quite often and in various forms associated with his Second Coming. In the case of the Sinai mosaic this association can be demonstrated in an indirect way. One of the peculiarities of the Metamorphosis (Pls. CIII, CXXXVI–CXXXVII), which is indeed surprising, is the absence of any indication of Mount Tabor, a feature so essential to the narrative and never omitted from later depictions of this scene. There is a passage in John Chrysostom's homily on the Metamorphosis in which he equates the vision on Mount Tabor with the Second Coming of Christ: "Thereafter he shall appear in the glory of the Father, not only with Moses and Elijah but with an unlimited host of angels, not with a cloud over his head, but surrounded by heaven." In this interpretation, Christ is appearing not on earth but in heaven, and this is the impression the mosaic artist tries to convey by omitting the mountain.

Most basic, of course, is the question of why the subject of the Metamorphosis was chosen at all, since for the eschatological idea other themes of equal significance could be and were chosen. It is, first of all, a rare subject for an Early Christian apse and only one parallel exists, the apse of San Apollinare in Classe in Ravenna where, however, the theme is treated pictorially and iconographically in a very different manner. In the Orthodox church the Metamorphosis is one of the twelve great feasts of the ecclesiastical year, and the reason for its inclusion in the cycle is dogmatic. One dogma in particular had the greatest impact on Byzantine art in general: the dogma of the two natures of Christ as formulated at the fourth Ecumenical Council of Chalcedon in 451. What better visualization of this dogma could there be than Christ's transfiguration from the human to the divine nature and then from the divine to the human before the very eyes of the apostles who had accompanied him to Mount Tabor?

That the conveying of the essence of this dogma to the beholder was indeed one of the main concerns of whoever designed the program of the mosaic is also apparent in other respects. The two medallions on the axis with the Christ figure are juxtaposed in such a way that the golden cross, set against three concentric strips, symbolizing the Trinity (Pls. CIII, CXXXVI–CXXXVII), alludes to the divine nature of Christ, while the bust of David (Pls. CXIX B, CLXX) alludes to the genealogy and thus to his human nature.

This idea of the two natures spills over into the triumphal arch where the sacrificial lamb in the central medallion (Pls. CXXII A, CLXXV) emphasizes the human nature of Christ and the golden cross set against the three concentric blue strips once more the divine. However, this is not the chief reason for the depiction of the symbolic lamb here. Primarily, the lamb has to be seen in context with the whole triumphal arch, i.e., in relation to the two angels who offer the scepter and orb (Pls. CXXII B, CXXIII B, CLXXVI–CLXXVII) and to the medallions of the Virgin and John the Baptist (Pls. CXXIV–CXXV, CLXXVI–CLXXVII, CLXXX–CLXXXI). This very grouping is known in Byzantine art as the *Deesis*, i.e., the Supplication in which the Virgin and John the Baptist appear as the intercessors for mankind, one for the New and the other the Old Dispensation. The concept is based on the Divine Liturgy, where in the Prayer of Intercession first the Virgin, then John the Baptist and after him the archangels are invoked, followed by the twelve apostles. Thus, the apostles of the Sinai mosaic have a double function: as witnesses of Christ's divine nature with regard to the Metamorphosis, and at the same time as intercessors in relation to the Deesis in the triumphal arch. The Deesis in the Sinai mosaic is the earliest one in existence and at the same time the only one in which Christ is depicted in the symbolic form of a lamb. After the Quinisext Council of 692 A.D. forbade the symbolic rendition of Christ, all later Deesis representations had to depict Him in human form, either standing or enthroned. Thus, the main emphasis of the triumphal arch is liturgical in comparison to the primarily eschatologic and dogmatic meaning of the Metamorphosis.

Furthermore, there are the two Moses scenes above the triumphal arch (Pls. CXXVI–CXXVII, CLXXXII–CLXXXV). Who, in looking at Moses loosening his sandals, would not be aware that right behind this wall there is the Chapel of the Burning Bush, the *locus sanctus* of the monastery? And who, seeing Moses receiving the tablets of the law, would not be reminded of the fact that through the clerestory windows one sees the high mountain of Ras Safsafa beyond which rises, though invisible from the monastery, the Gebel Musa whereon, according to tradition, Moses received the tablets? In the mosaic Moses is shown standing in a gorge which suggests that the artist was inspired by the serrated peaks of the actual locality. At the same time the topographical aspect is stressed not only by the presence of the various Moses figures but also by that of Elijah in the Metamorphosis. Halfway up the Moses mountain one passes by the Chapel of Elijah in which the *locus sanctus* is the cave of Horeb where he had been hiding (III Reg. XIX, 8). Yet this topographical connotation, self-evident as it may seem, was apparently not the primary reason for the choice of these scenes, since they occur also in the sanctuary of other Early Christian churches, e.g., in the choir of San Vitale in Ravenna. It is not even an invention of Christian art to relate these two Moses scenes to the focal point of the place of worship, because already in the third-century synagogue of Dura-Europos they flank the central panel above the niche for the Torah shrine, a place which takes the same central position in the Jewish rite as the apse does in the Christian.

The appearance of God to Moses is an epiphany just as the Metamorphosis is, and in this sense the Moses scenes foreshadow typologically an event in the life of Christ. Yet whereas in the Old Dispensation neither Moses nor Elijah was permitted to look upon the Lord but only to hear his voice (Ex. III, 4; Ex. XXXIII, 20ff.; III Reg. XIX, 13), the basic difference is that on Mount Tabor these two prophets did see the Lord in the manifestation of Christ and thus the representation of the Metamorphosis includes also an allusion to the dogma of the Incarnation. Obviously both topographic and typologic meanings are implied in the two Moses scenes.

Within the wreath of medallions, surrounding the Metamorphosis, a focal position is given the bust of David (Pls. CXIX B, CLXX). His purple chlamys and jewel-studded crown emphasize not only an imperial connotation in general, but show the prophet in the guise of the contemporary Byzantine emperor. Moreover, it will be noticed that David appears unbearded whereas normally he is depicted in Byzantine art with a beard and thus distinguished from King Solomon who, as a rule, wears no beard. Thus, it seems quite reasonable to assume that through such means of distinction the artist wanted to allude to Justinian, the founder of the Sinai monastery, who appears beardless also in two mosaics in Ravenna, the processional representation in San Vitale and the bust in S. Apollinare Nuovo. It is true that the mosaicist of Sinai did not try to individualize the imperial portrait like the Ravennate artists. Apparently, he wanted to convey primarily the impression of the biblical king and prophet and to allude to the living emperor in only a secondary manner. It may be recalled that according to the monastic tradition of Sinai Justinian is depicted in the mosaic, although the wrong figure is associated with the imperial founder, namely the one in the left medallion of the triumphal arch which depicts unquestionably John the Baptist (Pls. CXXIV, CLXXX). As so often, such legendary traditions bear a nucleus of truth, distorted as it may be in the course of time. We already mentioned the imperial aspect in connection with the Victory-Angels of the triumphal arch (Pls. CXXII B, CXXIII B, CLXXVI–CLXXVII). Thus, the emperor David is not the only feature of imperial iconography whereby we are made aware that Sinai is a foundation of the Emperor Justinian.

With these six layers of meaning—eschatologic, dogmatic, liturgic, topographic, typologic, and imperial—we may not have exhausted every facet of the rich and complex content of the Sinai mosaic, but we hope to have touched upon the most obvious and important. It is one of the great achievements of the artist in charge of the execution of this mosaic that he was able to find for such a complexity of content a clear and balanced composition which the beholder would be able to grasp immediately in its essentials.

Where did the artist or the artists come from who executed this mosaic? We have no record and are dependent only on inferences since no parallel is known today in the same style which might give a hint as to a possible workshop connection. We pointed out earlier that the chief master had an extraordinary facility for differentiating between various degrees of physical reality, in the case of divine figures avoiding human emotion altogether, and for the human figures rendering various modes of behavior from self-assured calm to exalted pathos. This power of expression is matched by the refinement of execution. Each garment gives the effect of an almost monochrome coloring when seen from a distance, but at close range shows a considerable number of subtle shades. What appears as black hair or the black border line of a garment is in reality deep purple, lightened at intervals by individual deep sea-green cubes (ordinary green cubes turned over) and amber cubes (gold ones reversed). Moreover, it will be noticed that especially in the upper zone (Pls. CXXVI–CXXVIII) the rows of gold cubes are slightly tilted so that the light reflects on them when one looks up from the floor of the church. Thus, a diffusion of sparkling light is calculated to be experienced by looking at the mosaic from a certain angle. It also should be observed that the Moses figures in the top zone are much taller than the figures of the Metamorphosis, a differentiation which has led some scholars to believe that the former must be dated later. Yet when one stands in front of the altar and looks up, one sees the two scenes at a very steep angle and the correcting eye reduces the tall proportions to normal size. These and other refinements undoubtedly point to a workshop which had developed them in a long tradition, established and continued by a highly trained team of craftsmen. We believe that in the time of Justinian only Constantinople could have supplied such highly trained craftsmen and, moreover, what could be more natural than that the emperor's personal patronage was responsible for sending these most skillful artists to the monastery of which he was the founder?

That even today a visitor receives such an unspoiled impression of the greatness of Justinianic mosaic art is due to the fact that the mosaic is in an excellent state of preservation and that it has been cleaned by our expedition. The comparatively dry air of the high mountains had much to do with the fact that, as a whole, damages are few and very minor. A restoration was made by a Russian artist in the middle of the nineteenth century, but fortunately he did not use cubes to fill in minor holes but only paint. It is not an exaggeration to say that every cube is in its original position, thus preserving the relief intended by the designer to diffuse the light and create the sparkling effect.

A major disaster was averted in 1959 when the Byzantine Institute of America, on the initiative of its director, Professor Paul Underwood, dispatched Mr. Ernest Hawkins and Mr. Carroll Wales to Sinai in order to prevent the collapse of the whole figure of Christ in the Metamorphosis, which was found to be detached from the vault of the apse. At more than fifty places, minute areas of the mosaic surface were temporarily removed in order that holes could be drilled into the underlying granite vault. Then copper clamps were inserted and new binding materials poured around them. Finally, the cubes were set back in place, not only in their original location, but also in the same profile, since in a good mosaic every cube is set at a slightly different angle in order to produce a diffused reflection of the light.

A second operation a year later, which Mr. Hawkins again executed with the help of some assistants, was the cleaning of the mosaic. In the course of centuries it had been covered not only with grime but other substances such as varnish and a kind of glue. After the cleaning the original colors came out not only more brightly and clearly but often different in actual hue from their former appearance when under the influence of the varnish. Nevertheless, it is well to remember when one looks at the bright color reproductions of this publication that these colors, while true, were photographed in the brilliant glare of electric floodlights. To the visitor standing in the bema they will appear more subdued and dimmed, giving the effect of a mystical glow which well may have been intended by the artist who created this mosaic.

Not long after the completion of the decoration of the bema with the precious materials of marble revetment and mosaic, the idea of expanding the program must have arisen. Since no room remained for additional representations in mosaic, the artist resorted to a very unusual and perhaps unique solution, namely that of painting two further scenes directly on the marble revetment in encaustic technique. In the preiconoclastic period this technique was almost exclusively reserved for icon painting, and we have in our present example a borderline case between two branches of painting which otherwise are clearly distinct in technique. These two panels are to be found on the pilasters left and right of the apse, so that the beholder can immediately relate them to the mosaic decoration and perceive them as part of an all-inclusive iconographic program for the sanctuary.

The panel on the pilaster to the left depicts the Sacrifice of Isaac (Pls. CXXX, CXXXII A, CXXXIII A, CLXXXVIII, CXCII A, CXCIII A), skillfully fitted into the narrow format. The altar is a tall structure, composed of three cubes in order to provide a platform for the kneeling Isaac and bring him within reach of Abraham, who grasps him by the hair and holds the daggerlike knife menacingly close. The patriarch's head is averted as if to avoid witnessing the intended slaughter with his own eyes. The Sacrifice of Isaac, already a favorite subject in Jewish art, as substantiated by several floor mosaics and by the fresco above the Torah shrine in the synagogue of Dura, was also frequently portrayed in Christian churches and especially in the altar room, where it is intended to prefigure Christ's sacrifice. The mosaic in the choir of San Vitale may be cited as a parallel of similar typologic significance.

St. Catherine's tomb (Pls. LXXXIV–LXXXV) stands in front of the pilaster at the right, and, in order to honor the titular saint of the church, this pilaster was covered in the eighteenth century by a somewhat older icon of St. Catherine, dressed as usual in imperial garb and set into a very heavy rococo marble frame whose exuberant ornamental forms were quite in disharmony with the grandiose simplicity of the early Christian apse decoration. I reasoned that in all probability there would be another encaustic painting underneath this late icon, i.e., a companion piece to the Sacrifice of Isaac. In 1960 the icon was temporarily removed and under it the lower part of a human figure became visible, executed in exactly the same encaustic technique as the Abraham panel. It depicted a soldier drawing a sword (Pl. CXC). The obvious implication was that this soldier should be another witness from the Old Testament and that the scene should be a further prefiguration of the death of Christ.

In 1963 the archbishop gave his gracious permission to have the rococo marble frame removed, a task performed with the greatest care by Mr. Hawkins. The total figure emerged with an inscription that left no doubt as to the subject matter of the scene (Pls. CXXXI, CXXXII B, CXXXIII B, CLXXXIX, CXCI, CXCII B, CXCIII B), which came as a great surprise and is unique in Early Christian art in general and in this context in particular. The soldier is Jephthah, who, before joining battle had made the vow that, if victorious, he would sacrifice whatsoever would come out of the door of his house (Jud. XI, 30 ff.). After his victory he returned to his house "and, behold, his daughter came out to meet him with timbrels and with dances." The Hebrew tradition of honoring vows left him no choice (Num. XXX, 2) and thus he felt obliged to sacrifice his only child. The encaustic panel actually depicts the gruesome slaughter of the little girl by her own father. She is kneeling on an altar constructed of three cubes like that of Isaac, while Jephthah,

dressed as a Roman soldier, holds her by the hair and, bending back her head, cuts her throat with his sword. The panel is surely by the same hand as the Abraham and Isaac panel and composed as a counterpart, the actions of both being oriented towards the center, i.e., toward the altar that stands between them. Without a doubt then, Jephthah's sacrifice must also be understood typologically as a prefiguration of Christ's sacrificial death. We know of no parallel for this, and it seems quite likely that this scene was not often, if ever, repeated in this context in Early Christian and medieval art.

Artistically, these panels are not only somewhat weaker than the Metamorphosis mosaic as far as the understanding of the organic structure of the human body is concerned, but also more ornamentalized in that Abraham's garment is covered with a more geometrical system of highlights and Isaac's tunic with an all-over pattern of circles. Apparently somewhat later than the mosaic and most likely belonging to the seventh century, these panels nevertheless are surely preiconoclastic and in all probability pre-Islamic.

Whether other buildings within the monastery, contemporary with its foundation, contained wall decorations can no longer be ascertained, since too many of them, especially some chapels, were destroyed and fell victim to later replacement. One need only mention that the building occupying the total length of the south wall is a modern concrete structure for which several old chapels had to make way. Yet it is precisely in the south wall that the only early fresco painting has survived. Right within the thickness of the wall there is a tiny chapel (Pl. IX), accessible from a modern concrete stairway, whose walls are decorated to the last inch with frescoes of architectural and ornamental design. A tunnel vault, parallel to the wall, is embellished with a design that imitates a coffered ceiling, the individual coffers being filled with rosettes and birds (Pls. CXXXV B-C, CXCVII B, CXCVIII), whereas the wall itself imitates a marble revetment (Pls. CXXXV A, CXCVI), interrupted at regular intervals by an arrangement of gray-marbled pilasters with capitals and bases above a dado in painted opus sectile. The imitations of marble slabs between the pilasters show veins forming symmetrical patterns so much like those of the actual marble plaques in the bema that one is tempted to date the frescoes into the same period, i.e., the time of Justinian. The little apse (Pls. CXXXIV B, CXCIV) shows, under a conch filled by a shell, a crux gemmata with pearl hangings, while the flat wall on the opposite, i.e., the western side (Pls. CXXXIV A, CXCV), by perspective design suggests a second niche. In this tiny chapel an Early Christian system of wall decoration survives which is still deeply steeped in the classical tradition.

17

With these frescoes we have completed our brief survey of the monumental paintings of the Justinianic era, executed in mosaic, fresco, and even encaustic technique, which will be discussed at greater length in the forthcoming text volume. However, the paintings dealt with so far do not exhaust all the works of representational art of this period which still exist within the walls of the monastery. Sinai is the only place in which early, i.e., pre-iconoclastic, icons are preserved in considerable number, among them some of the highest quality. Most of them were surely imported, i.e. brought as gifts, while others may have been made in the monastery itself. Among other works of the Justinianic period, there is a huge bronze cross bearing an inscription and two delicately engraved Moses scenes. Originally, it may have stood in front of the main altar on top of a chancel screen consisting of marble columns carrying a marble beam. These and other works of art of the preiconoclastic period will be published in later volumes.

Inscriptions

by
Ihor Ševčenko

Nearly two hundred inscriptions—on stone, wood, and movable objects—have been preserved within the walls or in the immediate vicinity of St. Catherine's monastery. Out of this impressive number, sixteen Greek inscriptions may be assigned to the earliest and most intriguing period in the monastery's history, that is, roughly the years between 500 and 700. Out of Sinai's very rich manuscript collection, nothing but a few scant fragments date from the first centuries of the monastery's existence. Even when we look for specific information about the site in other sources, reliably written in this general period, we come up with no more than three or four passages. In fact, the earliest writer describing the foundation of the monastery in some detail is the patriarch of Alexandria, Eutychius, who lived in the second half of the tenth century. Unfortunately, by his time the legendary elements of the story pushed the historical ones into the background.

With the scarcity of other sources of information, the early inscriptions assume a special significance for the student of the history of Sinai. The inscriptions on the beams of the basilica's roof (Pls. LXXX–LXXXI) remain our most precise evidence for the limiting dates (548–65) of the monastery's construction, since they mention Emperor Justinian (d. 565) as living, and his wife Theodora (d. 548) as deceased. The third beam inscription identifies the builder of the basilica: his name was Stephanus, he hailed from Aila (near today's Eilat in the Gulf of 'Aqaba), and he seems to have been both an architect and a deacon. The composite inscription on the apse mosaic (Pls. CLXXI–CLXXIII) says that this work was executed in the days of Longinus, priest and abbot—otherwise unknown —and by the effort of Theodore the Priest, "second in command"—a person as mysterious to us as Longinus. When it comes to chronology, however, we are on firmer ground. Both the palaeography and the formulae of the mosaic inscription securely date this impressive work of

art to the early period. Thus, in spite of doubts recently voiced, an epigrapher may assert with confidence that the mosaic is not later than 600. Other inscriptions provide information on early buildings in the monastery or in its surroundings. Thus, a newly discovered inscription on an arch over the steep path leading toward the summit of Sinai (to be reproduced later) indicates that it was built under the auspices of "Abba Johannes the Abbot"—perhaps the famous seventh-century abbot of Sinai, John Climacus himself.

However, early inscriptions may be pressed to yield yet more. Along with the scant literary sources, they help to retrace the everyday cultural horizon of sixth- and seventh-century Sinai and to assess the intellectual and linguistic equipment of its monks. The preserved early inscriptions are mostly Greek—although some of them must have been incised by non-Greeks—with a sprinkling of Armenian and Syriac ones and even one Nabatean text. The analysis of epigraphic formulae and of spelling errors shows that the horizons of Sinai were almost entirely limited to Egypt, Syria, and Palestine. Therefore, we might reasonably look for the sources of early Sinaitic art and architecture in these regions, keeping in mind, however, that individual movable objects could have reached the young monastery from the capital, or, for that matter, from any area in the Empire. In sum, the early inscriptions reflect the same world which we know from seventh-century popular literature dealing with Sinai, such as the stories attributed to Anastasius the Sinaite or those inserted by John Moschus into his *Pratum Spirituale*.

When it comes to the monks' intellectual equipment, the early inscriptions show little sophistication and are closer to stories by Anastasius and Moschus than even to the Ladder of Divine Ascent written by John Climacus on Sinai itself. Texts, both literary and epigraphical, give the impression that soon after the Arab conquest of the peninsula in the middle of the seventh century, Sinai was becoming the backwater which it was to remain until the beginning of the eleventh century.

Among the few inscriptions of any length, only two are free of spelling errors. One of these is the mosaic inscription, which may reflect the imported mosaicists' level of education; another, a slab protecting the relics of Sinai's Holy Fathers, who rest in the basilica's southeast chapel (Pl. CII D). The slab's text, hitherto misunderstood, commemorates the "four times ten" fathers (of Sinai) who had "imitated the baptism by blood of an equal number of Martyrs." This wording singularly reminds us of a story ascribed to one Ammonius, in which the figure of thirty-nine monks slaughtered by the Saracens—purportedly in the late fourth century—was rounded out when the lightly wounded monk Sabas joined the others in martyrdom "so that with me the number forty of Thy servants may be fulfilled." The story purports to be an eyewitness account of late fourth-century events; in fact,

it is later and must have been composed—perhaps by some learned Sinaitic monk—toward the end of the sixth century. Ammonius' "eyewitness" story so beguiled scholars that until quite recently, his account served as a basis for depicting the tribulations which Sinai's monks had supposedly undergone in 373 or about 400. Our marble plaque, dating from the late sixth century, seems thus to be an epigraphic *pendant* to literary fabrications undertaken roughly at the same time in order to provide the newly founded monastery—or at least its site—with martyrs of its own.

Among the sixteen earliest inscriptions which our expedition collected, five seem not to have been previously mentioned (Pls. CII B-C), the readings of seven have been modified—we hope improved (Pls. CII A 1–2, D), several inscriptions, including the three on the basilica's beams, have been fully uncovered for the first time (Pls. LXXX–LXXXI), and all have been permanently recorded.

The Church and Fortress

Moses Chapel on summit

Mount Sinai

The Monastery
of
Saint Catherine

PLATE II

General view of the Monastery from south. Gardens and charnel house on left

PLATE III

Monastery from northeast (cf. plan on Figure A)

PLATE IV

A. Southeast wall (left). Sixth–century construction with later buttresses and superstructure

B. Northeast wall. Outer face mostly later construction

PLATE V

A. Northwest wall (right). Sixth–century construction with later additions and buttresses

B. Southwest wall (right). Sixth–century construction with later buttresses and superstructure

PLATE VI

B. Sixth-century corner fragment (A)

A. Right half of northeast wall (Plate IV B). Incorporates fragments of sixth-century wall (B, C)

D. Interior face of northeast wall (partly sixth century) (Figure A no. 17)

C. Sixth-century fragment (A, center)

PLATE VII

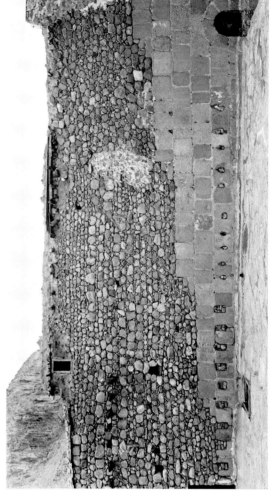

C. Crenellations (Plate IV A, left)

B. Latrine tower (Plate IV A, center; Figure A no. 22)

E. Interior face of A

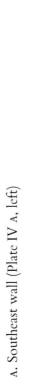

A. Southeast wall (Plate IV A, left)

D. Crenellations (Plate IV A, center)

PLATE VIII

B. Loophole under center hood of A

A. Center bay of southwest wall (Plate V B)

PLATE IX

B

A

A–B. Chapel above loophole (Plate VIII B, Figure A no. 28)

PLATE X

C

G

B

F

E

A

A–C. Hoods over loopholes in tower (Plate VIII A)

D–G. Hoods over loopholes at foot of southwest wall (Plate V B)

D

PLATE XI

B. Machicolation over main portal (Plate XII A)

E. Hood at right center of Plate XII A

A. Typical masonry; loopholes with and without hoods (Plate V B)

D

C

C–D. Hoods in A

PLATE XII

A. Northwest wall (Plate V A). At left, present entrance porch and blocked portal (Figure A nos. 1, 2)

B. Sixth-century portal in A

PLATE XIII

A. Present entrance porch (Plate XII A)

B. Porch (A) with second door closed

C. Porch (A) from inside; overhead, original postern arch

D. Inner door (to left in C; cf. Figure A no. 3)

PLATE XIV

Interior of fortress looking from entry across court and through vaulted passage to corner of church (Figure A nos. 3, 4, 5, 6)

PLATE XV

A. Entry of fortress (Figure A no. 3)

B. Entry of fortress seen from corner of church (cf. Plate XIV). To right, mosque and minaret; in foreground, steps to church (Figure A nos. 6, 7, 8)

PLATE XVI

Minaret and mosque (sixth-century hall) behind it (Figure A nos. 7, 8)

PLATE XVII

A. Mosque (sixth–century hall) through door at right center of Plate XVI; at top center, door of destroyed second story

B. Diagonal view in A; doors of destroyed second story and traces of its floor

PLATE XVIII

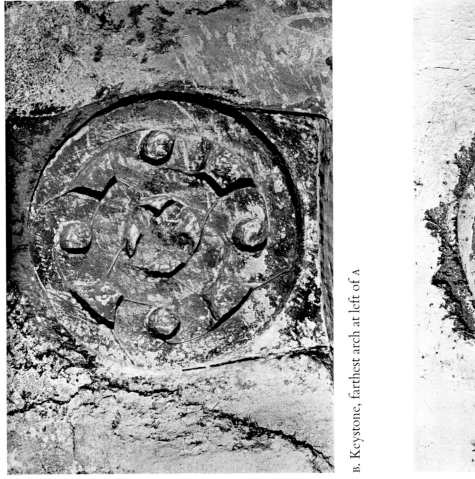

B. Keystone, farthest arch at left of A

C. Other face (east) of B

A. Antechamber to hall (Figure A no. 9)

PLATE XIX

B. Arches supporting floor of mosque (Plate XVII A)

D. Arches against outer wall of fortress, at far end of c

A. Arches supporting terrace in front of mosque (Plate XVI, right)

C. Arches in basement of fortress, southwest corner (Figure A no. 10)

PLATE XX

A. Arches and half tunnel vault (at rear) abutting northwest wall of fortress, in basement (to south of B)

B. Drain (Figure A no. 11)

PLATE XXI

A. Sixth-century kitchen and well (Figure A, under no. 12)

B. Sixth-century kitchen and oven (opposite view to A)

PLATE XXII

A. Front of oven (Plate XXI B)

B. Brick dome inside oven (A)

PLATE XXIII

A. Sixth-century vaulted storeroom adjoining kitchen (Plate XXI A)

B. Storeroom (A, opposite view); at rear, outer wall of fortress

PLATE XXIV

West façade and bell tower of church at right; mosque and minaret at left; steps to portal of church at center (Figure A no. 6)

PLATE XXV

West façade of church (Figure B). Sixth century except recent three-story campanile at left and portal at bottom left

PLATE XXVI

North flank of church at center; minaret at right (Figure A)

PLATE XXVII

A. West gable of church

B. Palmette on A

C. Palmette on A

PLATE XXVIII

A. Façade of church. North tower under recent campanile

B. South tower of façade

PLATE XXIX

A. Interior of south tower (Plate XXVIII B)

B. Interior of north tower (Plate XXVIII A) before removal of gallery over narthex (Plate XXXI B)

PLATE XXX

A. West façade of church (Plate XXV). Nave window (cf. Plate XC A)

B

B–D. West façade of church. Brackets

C

D

PLATE XXXI

A. South end of narthex (Plate XXV)

B. Church before removal, in 1959, of gallery over narthex (cf. Plate XXVI)

PLATE XXXII

A. Northwest corner of church, seen from Well of Moses (Figure A no. 13).
At left, north door and window of narthex. At right, base of minaret

B. Northwest corner of church at left (A) and sixth-century arch across passage

PLATE XXXIII

B. Detail of A (cf. Plate XC c)

A. North end of narthex (Plate XXXII A)

PLATE XXXIV

B. Sixth-century tower (A) under recent campanile

A. North side of church seen from passage (Figure A no. 14; cf. Plate XXXV, right side)

PLATE XXXV

Church from northeast (Figure B)

PLATE XXXVI

B. East end of church from south

A. East end of church

PLATE XXXVII

B. Sixth-century tower (cf. A and Plate XXV)

A. South side of church. Nave flanked by aisle, side chapels (under skylights) and passage (Figure A no. 15)

PLATE XXXVIII

B. South side of church at end of passage in A. Coping and wall below, sixth century

C. Southeast corner of church (embedded, center). Left, cf. B. Right, cf. Plate XXXIX

A. Passage along south side of church; sixth-century tower at left (Plate XXXVII B). Medieval refectory in center (Figure A no. 23)

PLATE XXXIX

A. Burning Bush Chapel (Figure B, 1)

B. East end of church (Plate XXXVI A)

PLATE XL

A. Southeast corner of church (cf. Plate XXXVIII c)

B. Northeast corner of church (Plate XXXIX B)

PLATE XLI

A. Window under gable (Plates XXXV, CXXIX A)

B. Window of apse (Plates XXXV, LXXXVIII)

C

D

C–D. Brackets (Plate XXXV)

PLATE XLII

A. Northeast corner of church (Plate XXXV)

B

C

B–C. Brackets on east gable (Plate XLI C–D)

D. Bracket on aisle (A, center)

PLATE XLIII

Nave of church seen through portal from narthex (Figure B). Sixth-century nave arcades, walls,
carvings on ceiling beams, and portal (Plate XLVI)

PLATE XLIV

B. Portal of nave

A. Narthex (Figure B, A). Left to right: porch door; north door; nave portal

PLATE XLV

B. South end of narthex. Left to right: nave portal; window (opened later); porch door

A. Portal of nave

PLATE XLVI

Portal from narthex to nave (Plate XLIII)

PLATE XLVII

Details of nave portal: A. Wooden lintel

B. Left capital

C. Right capital

D. Cross on A

E. Small capital

F. Handle

G

H

G–H. Left pilaster

I

J

I–J. Right pilaster

PLATE XLVIII

A

B

C

D

Panels of nave portal (Plate XLVI), left half: A–B. Top panels; C–D. Second row

PLATE XLIX

A

B

C

D

Panels of nave portal, right half: A–B. Top panels; C–D. Second row

PLATE L

A

B

C

D

Panels of nave portal, left half: A–B. Third row; C–D. Fourth row

PLATE LI

A

B

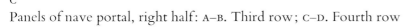

C

D

Panels of nave portal, right half: A–B. Third row; C–D. Fourth row

PLATE LII

A

B

C

D

Panels of nave portal, left half: A–B. Fifth row; C–D. Sixth row

PLATE LIII

A

B

C

D

Panels of nave portal, right half: A–B. Fifth row; C–D. Sixth row

PLATE LIV

A

B

C

D

Panels of nave portal: A–B. Two bottom panels of left half; C–D. Two bottom panels of right half

PLATE LV

Portal from narthex to nave. Face toward nave (cf. Plate XLVI)

PLATE LVI

Details of nave portal: A. Outer lintel (Plate XLVI); B. Inner lintel (Plate LV); C–N. Panels toward nave, first three rows from top (Plate LV)

PLATE LVII

Details of nave portal: A–P. Panels toward nave, four lower rows (continued from Plate LVI)

PLATE LVIII

South aisle of church, looking southeast (Figure B, D)

PLATE LIX

South aisle of church, looking west (cf. Plate LVIII)

PLATE LX

North aisle of church, looking east (Figure B, c)

PLATE LXI

A

B

C

D

Column bases under nave arcades. South side (Plate LIX):
A–C. First three bases from west.

North side (Plate LX): D. Seventh base from west

PLATE LXII

B

D

A

C

Capitals under nave arcades. North side: A–D. First four capitals from west

PLATE LXIII

B

D

A

C

Capitals under nave arcades. North side (continued from Plate LXII): A–D. Fifth through eighth (last) capital from west

PLATE LXIV

B

D

A

C

Capitals under nave arcades. South side (Plates LVIII, LIX): A–D. First four capitals from west

PLATE LXV

B

D

A

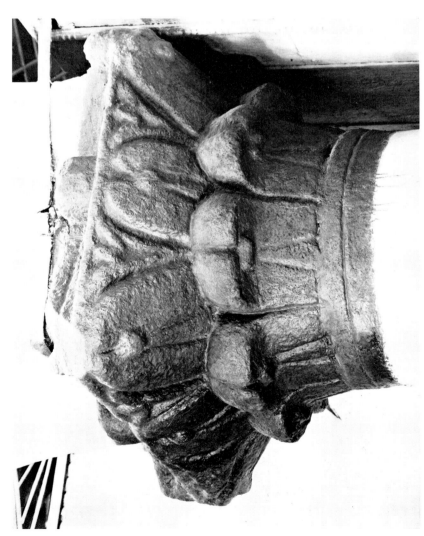

C

Capitals under nave arcades. South side (continued from Plate LXIV): A–D. Fifth through eighth (last) capital from west

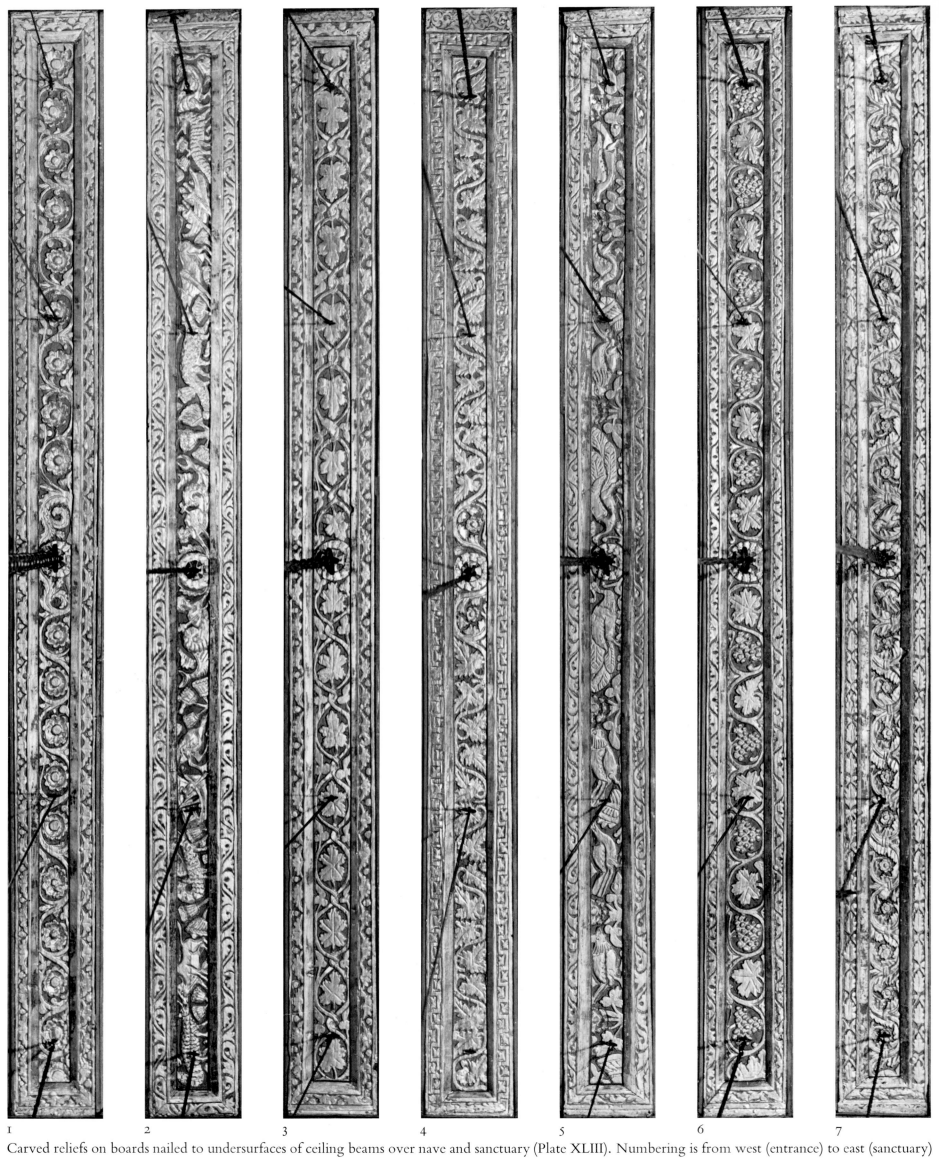

1   2   3   4   5   6   7

Carved reliefs on boards nailed to undersurfaces of ceiling beams over nave and sanctuary (Plate XLIII). Numbering is from west (entrance) to east (sanctuary)

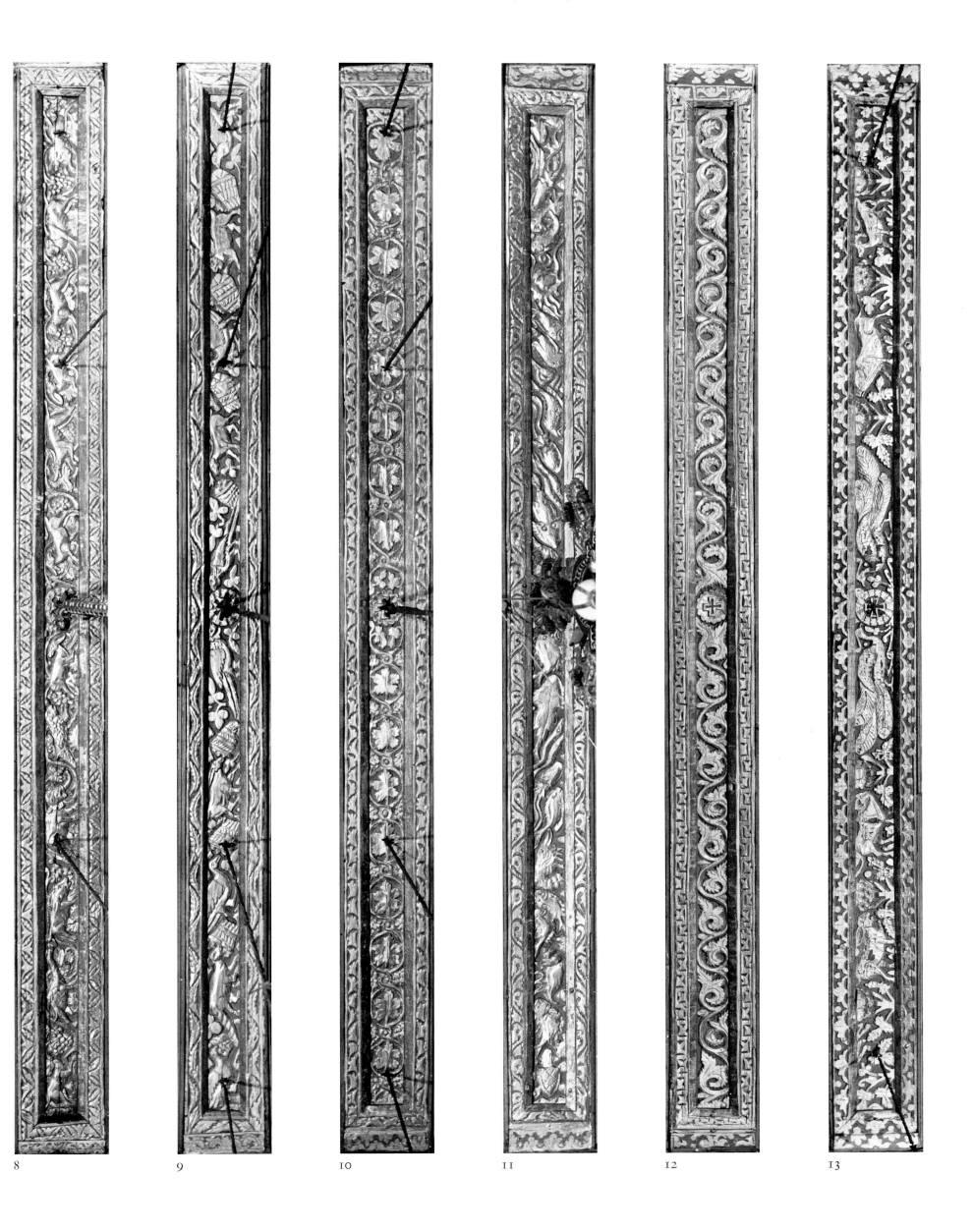

8   9   10   11   12   13

PLATE LXVIII

A

B

A–B. Details from Plate LXVI, beam no. 2

PLATE LXIX

A

B

A–B. Details from Plate LXVI, beam no. 2 (continued)

PLATE LXX

A

B

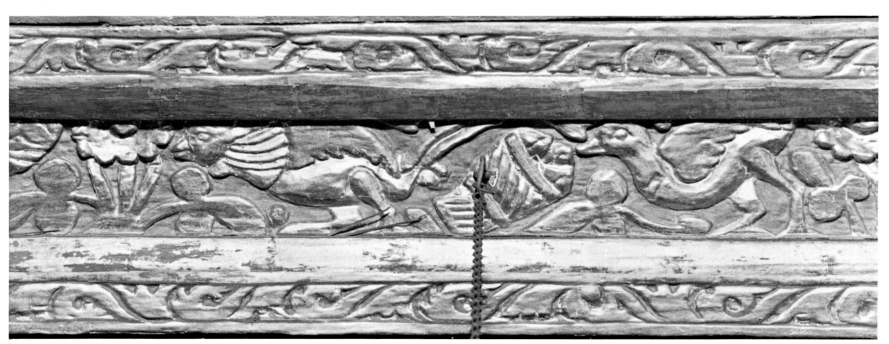

C

A–C. Details from Plate LXVI, beam no. 5

PLATE LXXI

A

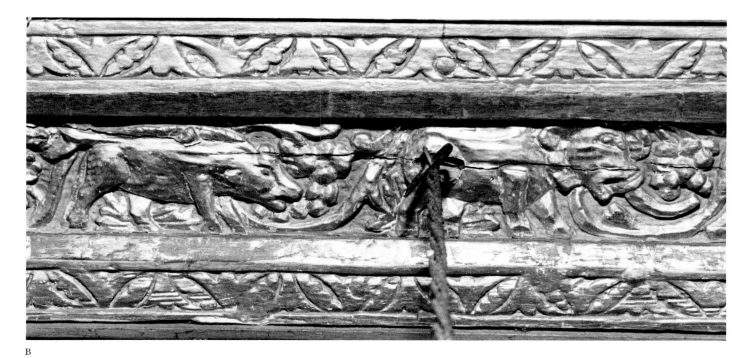

B

C

A–C. Details from Plate LXVII, beam no. 8

PLATE LXXII

A

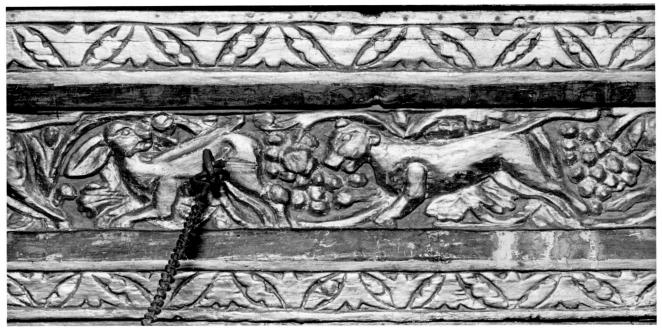

B

C

A–C. Details from Plate LXVII, beam no. 8 (continued)

PLATE LXXIII

A

B

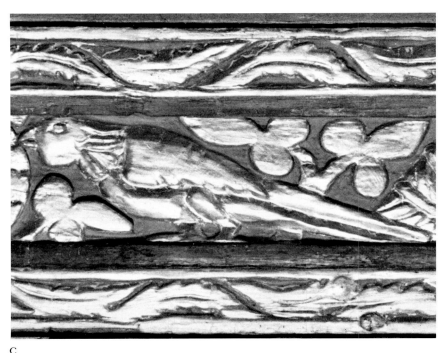

C

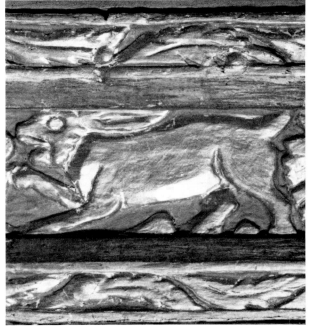

D

A–D. Details from Plate LXVII, beam no. 9

PLATE LXXIV

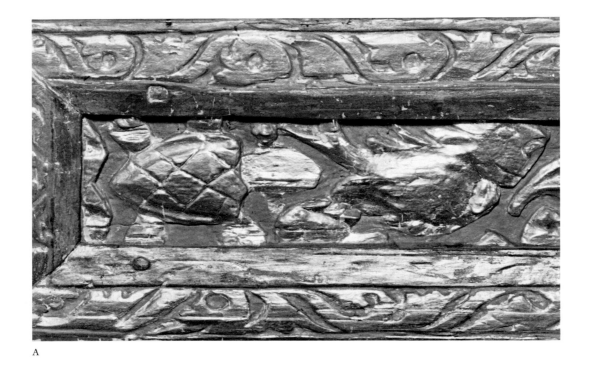

A

B

C

A–C. Details from Plate LXVII, beam no. 11

PLATE LXXV

A

B

C

A–C. Details from Plate LXVII, beam no. 11 (continued)

PLATE LXXVI

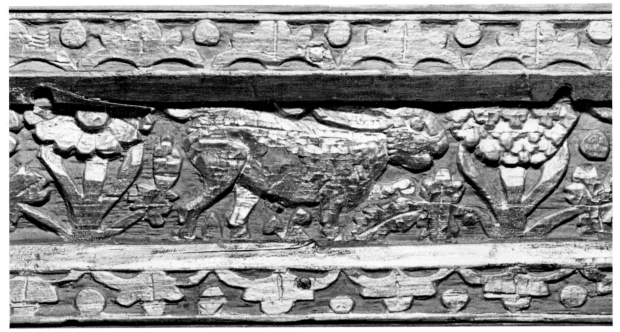

A

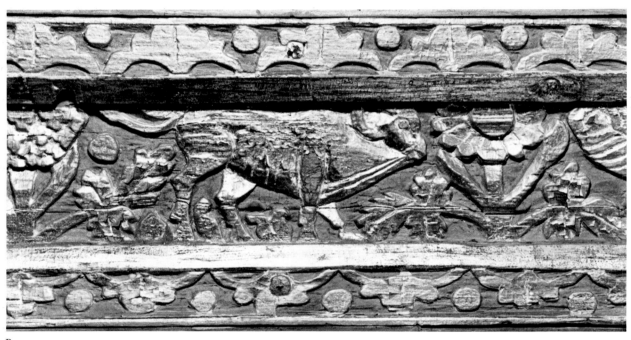

B

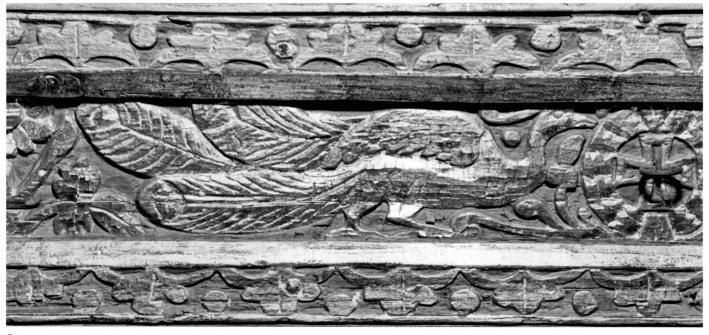

C

A–C. Details from Plate LXVII, beam no. 13

PLATE LXXVII

A

B

C

A–C. Details from Plate LXVII, beam no. 13 (continued)

PLATE LXXVIII

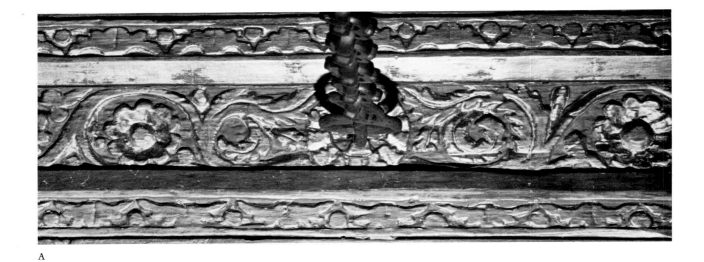

A

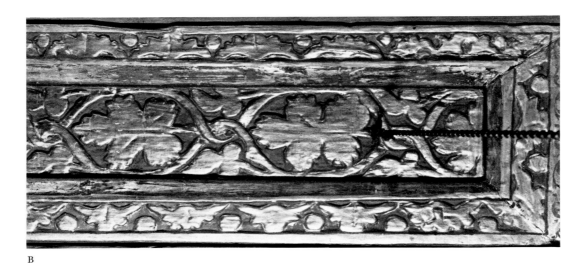

B

C

D

Details of beams (Plate LXVI): A. Beam no. 1; B. Beam no. 3; C. Beam no. 4; D. Beam no. 6

PLATE LXXIX

A

B

C

D

Details of beams (Plates LXVI–LXVII): A–B. Beam no. 7
(on right of B is later patching strip); C. Beam no. 10; D. Beam no. 12

A. Vertical board attached to east face of ceiling beam no. 1 (Plate LXVI); photo

+ΚΕΘΟΟΟΦΘΕΙΟΕΝΤШΤΟΠШΤΟΥΤΟΥΤШΟ
ΤΥΡΙΟΥΔΙΚ°ΚΑΙΤΕΚΤΟΝΑΔΙΛΗΟΙΟΝΚΑΙΝΟΝΝΑ

B. Same; Latex mold

C. Vertical board attached to ceiling beam no. 7 (inscription faces west); photo

+ΥΠΕΡΗΝΗΜΜΗΟΚΑΝΑ   ΠΑΥΟΕШΟΤΗΟΓΕΝΑ

D. Same; Latex mold

E. Vertical board attached to ceiling beam no. 8 (inscription faces west); photo

+ΥΠΕΡΟШΤΗΡΙΑΟ   ΤΟΥΕΥΟΕΒΗΜШΝ

F. Same; Latex mold

G. Vertical board attached to ceiling beam no. 1, detail; photo

H. Vertical board attached to ceiling

ΟΝΚΑΙΕΛΕΗΣΟΝΤΟΝΔΟΥΛΟΥΣΤΕΦΑΝΟΝΗΑΡ
ΑΝΑΠΑΥΣΟΝΤΑΣΨΥΧΑΣΤΩΝΤΕΚΝΩΝΑΥΤΟΥΓΕΟΡΓ

m no. 7, detail; photo   1. Vertical board attached to ceiling beam no. 8, detail; photo

PLATE LXXXII

A. Roof trusses (sixth century) above nave and sanctuary, looking west (cf. Plate XLIII). Ceiling panels are later

B. Detail of A, left side

C. Roof ridge

PLATE LXXXIII

A. Roof truss, seventh from west

B. Detail of truss, eighth from west, north end

PLATE LXXXIV

Sanctuary of church (Figure B, E). Tomb of St. Catherine beyond altar

PLATE LXXXV

Tomb of St. Catherine, incorporating some sixth-century elements (Plates LXXXVI B, LXXXIX B). South aisle at rear

PLATE LXXXVI

A. Chancel panel (Plate LXXXIV)

B. Chancel panel and capital under St. Catherine's tomb, facing south aisle (Plate LXXXV)

PLATE LXXXVII

A. Stone altar table (sixth century?) within later wood structure (Plate LXXXIV)

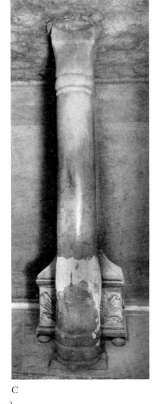

B

C

D

B–D. Five columnar supports and base of altar table (above)

PLATE LXXXVIII

Window at center of apse (Plates LXXXIV, XLI B). Sixth-century marble revetment and throne (altered later)

PLATE LXXXIX

A. Marble revetment in apse (Plate LXXXVIII)

B. Marble capital under St. Catherine's tomb (Plate LXXXVI B)

PLATE XC

A. Window, west end of nave (Plate XXX A). Glazing later

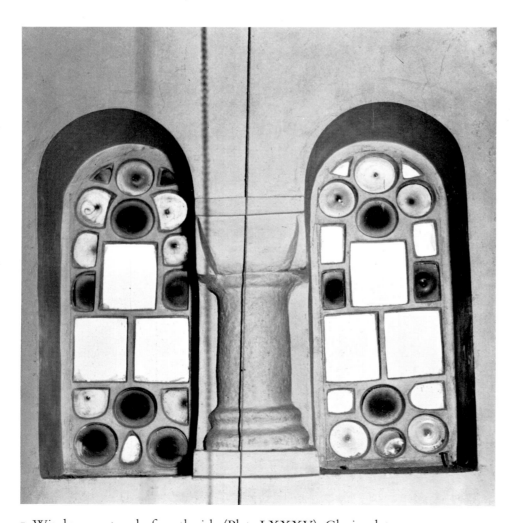

B. Window, east end of south aisle (Plate LXXXV). Glazing later

C. Window, north end of narthex
(Plate XXXIII B). Glazing later

PLATE XCI

A

B

C

D

A–D. Aisle windows

PLATE XCII

B. Chapel of SS. Cosmas and Damian, under southwest tower (Figure B, Q)

A. Chapel of St. Marina, under northwest tower (Figure B, N)

PLATE XCIII

B. Chapel of St. Simeon Stylites (Figure B, P)

A. Chapel of SS. Constantine and Helen (Figure B, M)

PLATE XCIV

B. Bronze sheathed door from south aisle to Chapel of
the Forty Martyrs (Plate XCVI A)

A. Bronze sheathed door from north aisle to Chapel of
St. James the Less (Plate XCVI B)

PLATE XCV

C

B

A

G

F

E

D

Bronze fittings on doors (Plate XCIV): A, D, E, F on north door; B, C, G on south door

PLATE XCVI

B. Door from Chapel of St. James the Less to north aisle (Plate XCIV A)

A. Door from Chapel of the Forty Martyrs to south aisle (Plate XCIV B)

PLATE XCVII

A–J. Wood panels of door from Chapel of the Forty Martyrs to the south aisle (Plate XCVI A)

PLATE XCVIII

B. Chapel of St. James the Less (A). Door to Chapel of Burning Bush (Plate C)

A. Chapel of St. James the Less (Figure B, J)

PLATE XCIX

B. Apse of Chapel of the Forty Martyrs (A)

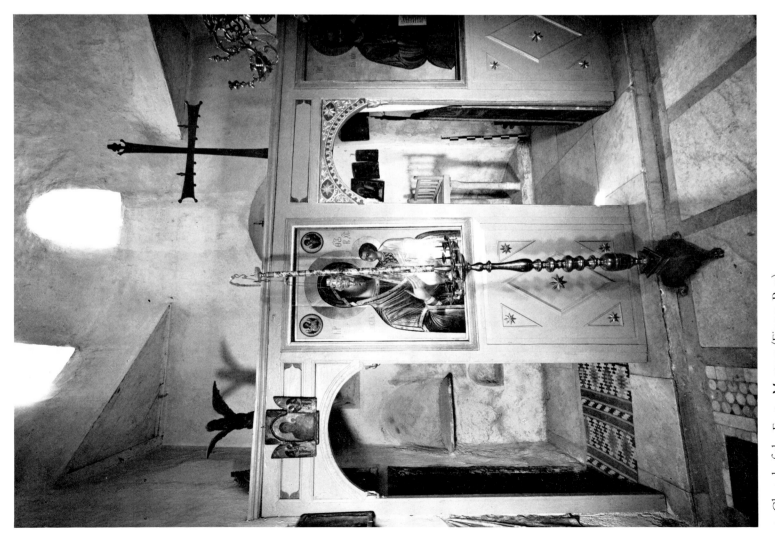

A. Chapel of the Forty Martyrs (Figure B, K)

PLATE C

Chapel of Burning Bush (Figure B, 1). Left, door from Chapel of St. James the Less (Plate XCVIII B). Right, site of Burning Bush (Plate CI)

PLATE CI

A. Chapel of Burning Bush (Plate C). Slab under altar on site of Burning Bush

B. Chapel of Burning Bush. Slab (A) with metal cover raised

PLATE CII

A. Refectory. Lintel over the NW window, 2 blocks of granite. Inscription on behalf of Stephen the Archdeacon, Gerontius the priest of St. Theodore, and Samuel the Monk, lapidary, with quotations from Ps. 112 (113): 7.

B. Storage room under old Library. E jamb of pointed arch, door lintel formerly in the "Martyrium" of St. Stephen. Latex mold.

C. Old Library. Museum room, S wall, block of granite. Kanathos invokes the help of "one God" for himself and children. Latex mold.

D. Basilica. Chapel of the Holy Fathers, marble slab immured in S wall. Invocation to the Forty Martyrs of Sinai. Latex mold.

The Mosaics and the Wall Paintings

PLATE CIII

Transfiguration

PLATE CIV

Christ

PLATE CV

Head of Christ

PLATE CVI

Elijah

PLATE CVII

Moses

PLATE CVIII

Head of Elijah

PLATE CIX

Head of Moses

PLATE CX

John

PLATE CXI

James

PLATE CXII

Head of John

PLATE CXIII

Head of James

PLATE CXIV

Peter

PLATE CXV

Head of Peter

PLATE CXVI

B. Paul. First at right of summit cross

A. Andrew. First at left of summit cross

PLATE CXVII

B. Matthew. Fourth, right

A. James. Fourth, left

PLATE CXVIII

B. Malachi. Third, left

A. Daniel. First from left at bottom

PLATE CXIX

B. David. Bottom, center

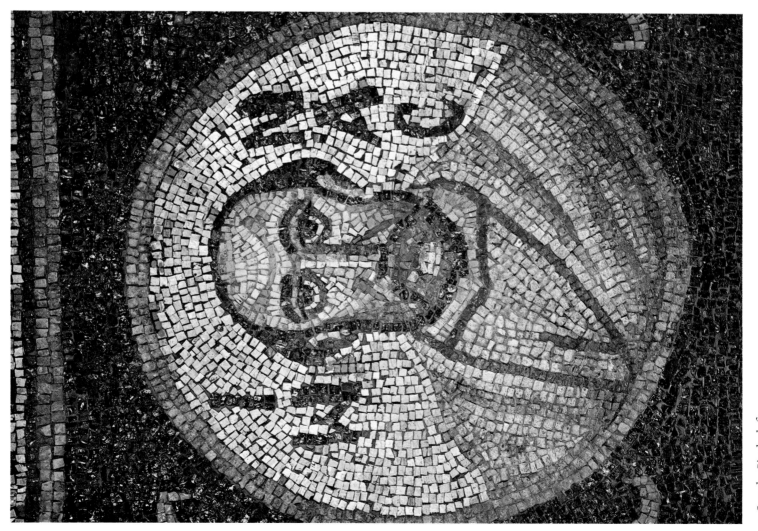

A. Jonah. Sixth, left

PLATE CXX

John the Deacon. Corner, left

PLATE CXXI

Longinus the Abbot. Corner, right

PLATE CXXII

A. The Lamb of God, at summit of Triumphal Arch
(Plate CIII)

B. Flying Angel and medallion of John the Baptist

PLATE CXXIII

A. Head of Flying Angel

B. Flying Angel and medallion of the Virgin

PLATE CXXIV

John the Baptist

PLATE CXXV

Virgin

PLATE CXXVI

Moses Loosening his Sandals

PLATE CXXVII

Moses Receiving the Tablets of the Law

PLATE CXXVIII

B. Head of Moses. Detail from Receiving the Tablets of the Law

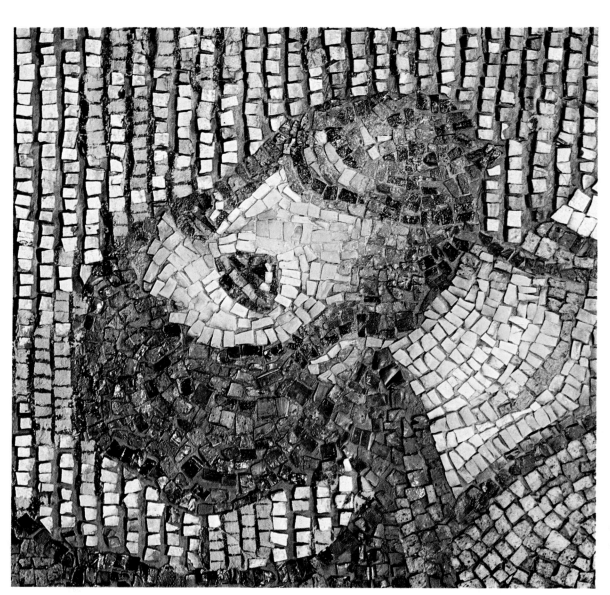

A. Head of Moses. Detail from Loosening his Sandals

PLATE CXXIX

A. Column above the Triumphal Arch

B. Section of ornamental border next to medallion of John the Baptist (Plate CXXII B)

PLATE CXXX

Encaustic painting on marble pilaster left of the apse. The Sacrifice of Isaac

PLATE CXXXI

Encaustic painting on marble pilaster right of the apse.
The Sacrifice of Jephthah's Daughter

PLATE CXXXII

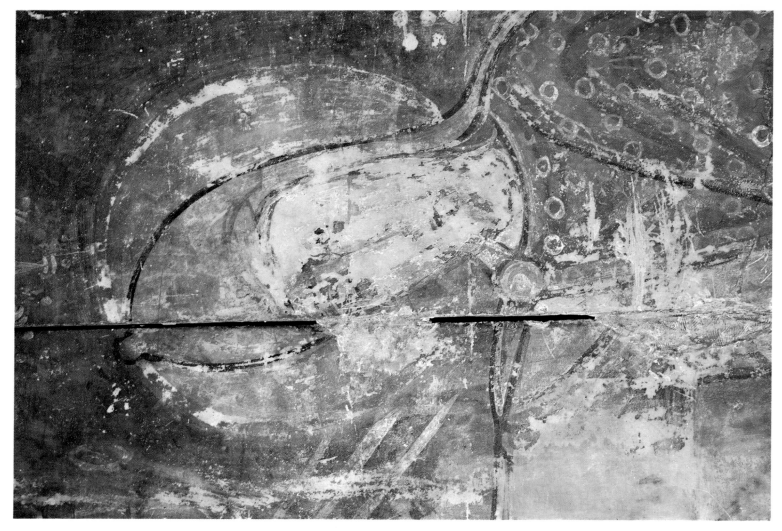

B. Head of Jephthah

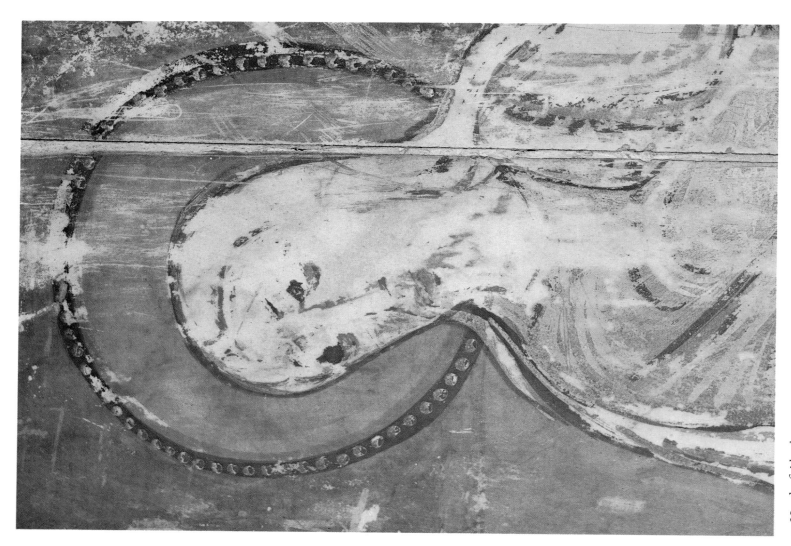

A. Head of Abraham

PLATE CXXXIII

B. Jephthah's Daughter

A. Isaac Kneeling upon the Altar

PLATE CXXXIV

B. View into the apse at the east end

A. View into the niche at the west end

Fresco decoration of the Chapel within the south wall (Plate IX)

PLATE CXXXV

B. Tunnel vault. Detail

C. Tunnel vault. Detail

A. System of wall decoration opposite the entrance

Fresco decoration of the Chapel within the south wall (Plate IX)

Transfiguration

PLATE CXXXVIII

Christ. Before restoration and cleaning

PLATE CXXXIX

Christ

PLATE CXL

Bust of Christ

PLATE CXLI

Head of Christ

PLATE CXLII

Elijah

PLATE CXLIII

Moses

PLATE CXLIV

Head of Elijah

PLATE CXLV

Head of Moses

PLATE CXLVI

John

PLATE CXLVII

James

PLATE CXLVIII

Head of John

PLATE CXLIX

Head of James

PLATE CL

Peter

PLATE CLI

Head of Peter

PLATE CLII

The Cross-disk in the summit. Before cleaning

PLATE CLIII

B. Thaddaeus and Mathias. Fifth and sixth, right. Before cleaning

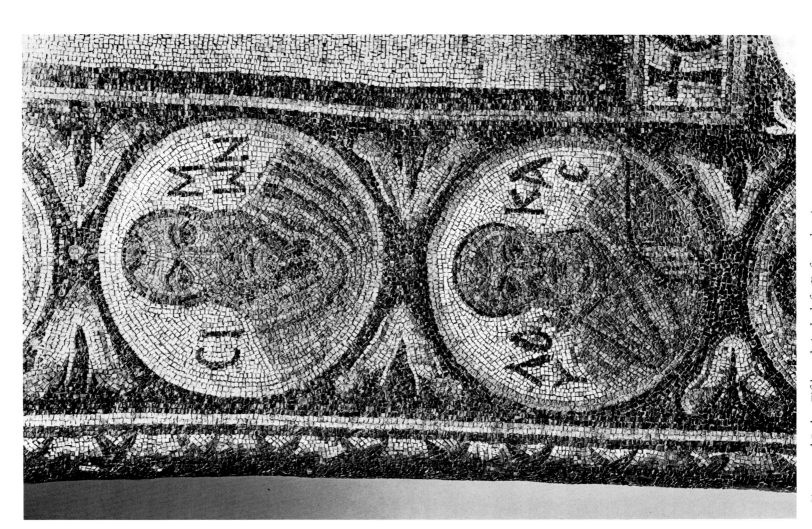

A. Simon and Luke. Fifth and sixth, left. Before cleaning

PLATE CLIV

B. Paul. First at right of summit cross

A. Andrew. First at left of summit cross

PLATE CLV

B. Philip. Second, right

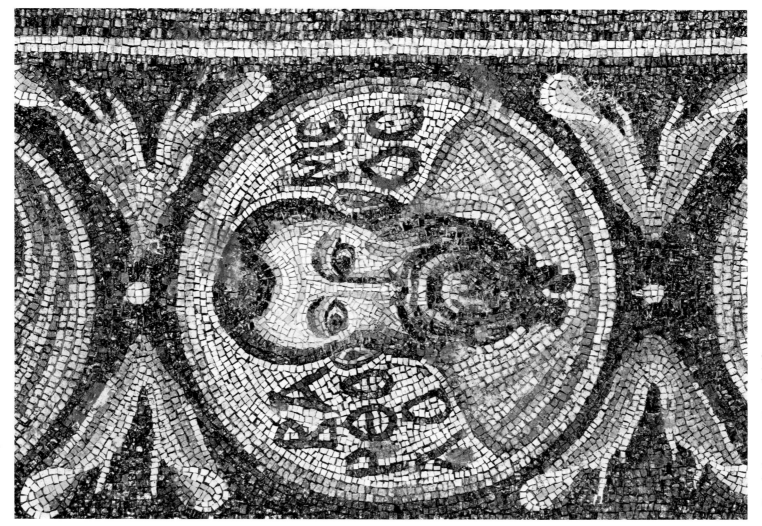

A. Bartholomew. Second, left

PLATE CLVI

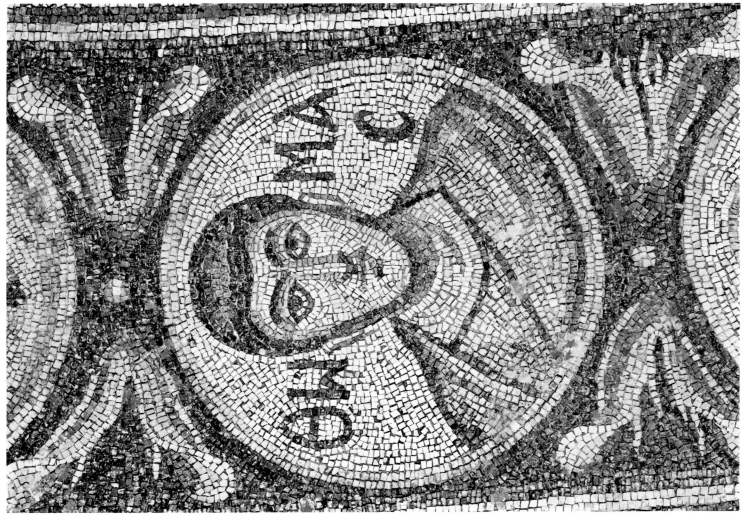

B. Thomas. Third, right

A. Mark. Third, left

PLATE CLVII

B. Matthew. Fourth, right

A. James. Fourth, left

PLATE CLVIII

B. Thaddaeus. Fifth, right

A. Simon. Fifth, left

PLATE CLIX

B. Matthias. Sixth, right

A. Luke. Sixth, left

PLATE CLX

John the Deacon. Corner, left

PLATE CLXI

Longinus the Abbot. Corner, right

PLATE CLXII

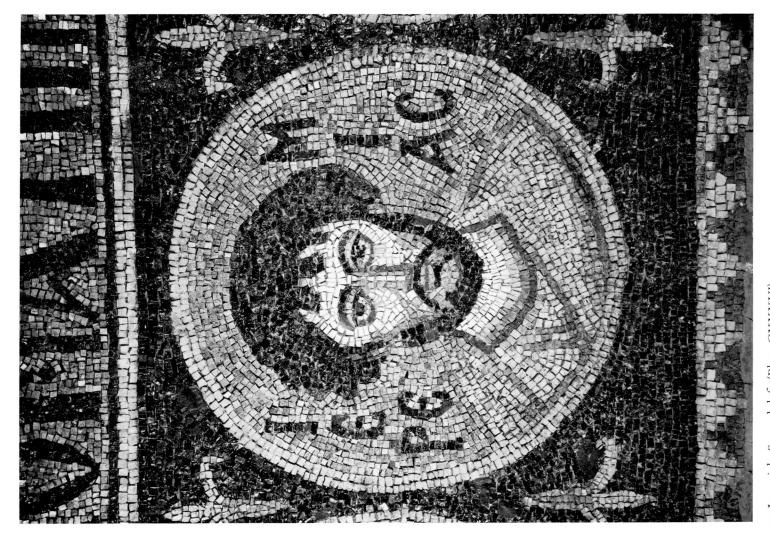

B. Jeremiah. Second, left (Plate CXXXVI)

A. Daniel. First from left at bottom (Plate CXXXVI)

PLATE CLXIII

A. Ezekiel. First from right at bottom (Plate CXXXVII)

B. Isaiah. Second, right (Plate CXXXVII)

PLATE CLXIV

B. Haggai. Fourth, left (Plate CXXXVI)

A. Malachi. Third, left (Plate CXXXVI)

PLATE CLXV

A. Zechariah. Third, right (Plate CXXXVII)

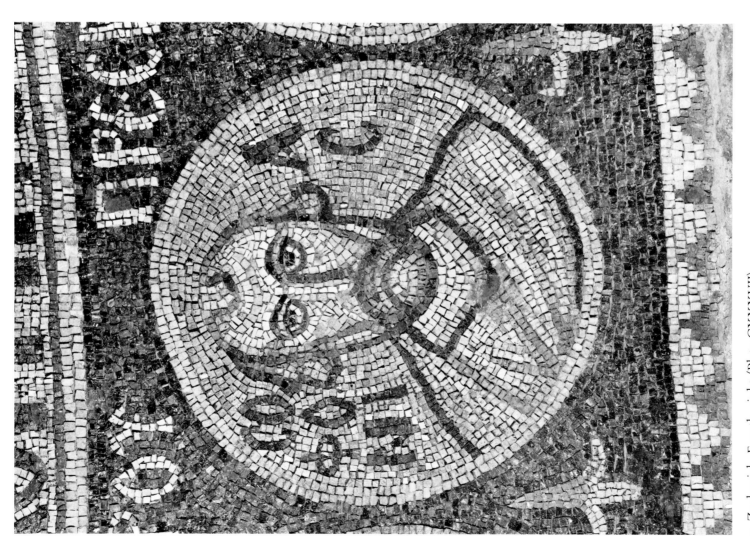

B. Zephaniah. Fourth, right (Plate CXXXVII)

PLATE CLXVI

B. Jonah. Sixth, left (Plate CXXXVI)

A. Habakkuk. Fifth, left (Plate CXXXVI)

PLATE CLXVII

A. Nahum. Fifth, right (Plate CXXXVII)

B. Obadiah. Sixth, right (Plate CXXXVII)

PLATE CLXVIII

B. Amos. Eighth, left (Plate CXXXVI)

A. Joel. Seventh, left (Plate CXXXVI)

PLATE CLXIX

A. Micah. Seventh, right (Plate CXXXVII)

B. Hosea. Eighth, right (Plate CXXXVII)

PLATE CLXX

David. Bottom, center (Plate CXXXVII)

PLATE CLXXI

A. The primary dedicatory inscription below the Transfiguration

B

C

D

B–D. The secondary dedicatory inscription above the right Prophet medallions

A

B

C

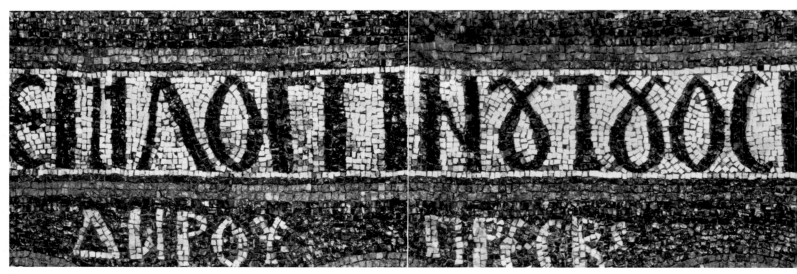

D

A–D. The primary dedicatory inscription

ΦΟΡΗCΑΝΤ

Ι Ο ΔΗΘΕΟ

PLATE CLXXIV

Triumphal Arch with the Lamb of God, two angels, John the Baptist, and the Virgin. Above, two Moses scenes

PLATE CLXXV

B

A

A–B. The Lamb of God. Before and after cleaning (Plate CLXXIV)

PLATE CLXXVI

Flying Angel and medallion of John the Baptist (Plate CLXXIV)

PLATE CLXXVII

Flying Angel and medallion of the Virgin (Plate CLXXIV)

PLATE CLXXVIII

Head of the left Angel (Plate CLXXVI)

PLATE CLXXIX

Head of the right Angel (Plate CLXXVII)

PLATE CLXXX

John the Baptist (Plate CLXXVI)

PLATE CLXXXI

Virgin (Plate CLXXVII)

PLATE CLXXXII

Moses Loosening his Sandals (Plate CLXXIV)

PLATE CLXXXIII

Moses Receiving the Tablets of the Law (Plate CLXXIV)

PLATE CLXXXIV

Moses Loosening his Sandals

PLATE CLXXXV

Moses Receiving the Tablets of the Law

PLATE CLXXXVI

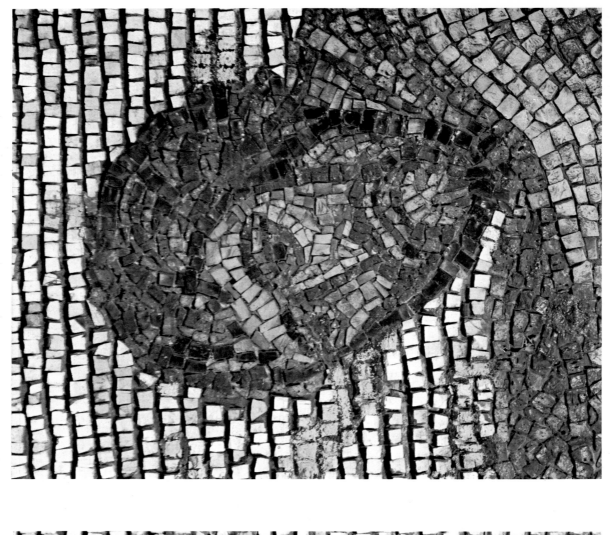

B. Head of Moses. From Receiving the Tablets of the Law (Plate CLXXXV)

A. Head of Moses. From Loosening his Sandals (Plate CLXXXIV)

PLATE CLXXXVII

Column above the Triumphal Arch

PLATE CLXXXVIII

Encaustic painting on marble pilaster left of apse. The Sacrifice of Isaac

PLATE CLXXXIX

Encaustic painting on marble pilaster right of apse. The Sacrifice of Jephthah's Daughter

PLATE CXC

The Jephthah scene before the removal of the late marble frame

PLATE CXCI

The Sacrifice of Jephthah's Daughter

PLATE CXCII

B. Head of Jephthah

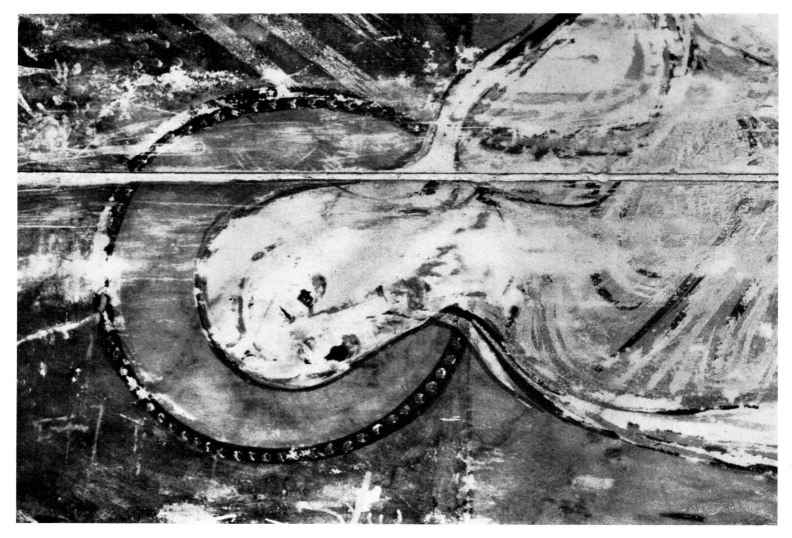

A. Head of Abraham

PLATE CXCIII

B. Jephthah's Daughter kneeling upon altar

A. Isaac kneeling upon altar

PLATE CXCIV

Fresco decoration of the Chapel within the south wall. View into the apse at the east end

PLATE CXCV

Fresco decoration of the Chapel within the south wall. View into the niche at the west end

PLATE CXCVI

Fresco decoration of the Chapel within the south wall. System of decoration opposite the entrance

PLATE CXCVII

A. The Cross over the niche at the west end

B. The tunnel vault

Fresco decoration of the Chapel within the south wall

PLATE CXCVIII

A

B

A–B. Details from the tunnel vault

Fresco decoration of the Chapel within the south wall

Book design by
QUENTIN FIORE

Plates by Schwitter Ltd. Basel
Composed and printed by Basler Druck- und Verlagsanstalt Basel
Binding by Max Grollimund Basel

WITHDRAWN